With Every Goodbye

If you are brave enough to say goodbye,
life will reward you with a new hello

Karin Jarvis

First Published in 2024 by Karin Jarvis

National Library of Australia Cataloguing-in-Publication data:

ISBN-13: (paperback edition) 978-1-7635788-0-7

ISBN-13: (e book)

Dedication

This book is dedicated to my parents, Anna and Harald Lorek who were brave enough to say goodbye to their homeland in Germany, to seek a new hello in Australia. Thanks to you, life has rewarded me richly with opportunities to do and be whatever I choose.

Table of Contents

Foreword

I was surprised, yet honoured when Karin asked me to write the foreword for this book.

To set the record straight, in some people's eyes I may be famous or infamous in the Mandurah community for the outlandish things I do, such as dressing up as Where's Wally to promote businesses and events, taking a Boom Box speaker on the train to get commuters up dancing after concerts in Perth, my avid social media commentaries or my array of voluntary positions over the years. All of which I do to assist in connecting a disconnected society. It has also, inadvertently, brought me notoriety over the years. I guess being awarded 2024 Mandurah Australia Day Citizen of the Year for the contributions I've made to the community has given me some fame as well.

I told Karin that when I read a book, if it does not grab my attention in the first chapter then the book would be put down, never to be opened again. I am thrilled to say that Karin's book captivated me from start to finish. Her writing ability is second to none. The way she described events that had happened in her life, the good, the bad and the ugly had my imagination believing I was walking in her shoes. There is the old saying 'you cannot judge a book by its cover.' That saying can be used to describe Karin. Her hard work, her planning, her inner grit, and determination have brought her and her family to where they are today.

I hope you enjoy reading Karin's book as much as I did. I wish her and her family all the happiness in the world, whatever paths they all choose to take.

I encourage Karin to continue to write more books for the world to enjoy.

Lisa Kelly
Mandurah's Citizen of The Year 2024

Preface

Are we the masters of our own destiny? Are our lives the sum of our formed beliefs, choices, and desires? Are we here to experience life, for better or for worse, to learn, and to discover our own truths? Did we come to Planet Earth to flounder from one mistake to the next until we discover the light? Are our lives already mapped out for us by an unknown deity?

Are we really born just so evil that we need to be rescued by a divine being? Is it our sole duty to serve others at the cost of our own happiness or is there perhaps a healthier balance to be found?

From an early age the unspoken message was to believe what we are told. Unquestioning obedience becomes the basis of our childhood. We feared punishment from an angry parent, a furious God, or a disappointed superior. Most of our training for life is absorbed before we are 7 years old, initially by our parents rehashing what they learnt, as they were instructed by their parents. And so, the chain of watered down truths, tales, falsities, and fears are passed onto the next generation. The process continues via school, peers, governments, churches, and television.

At what point do you come to the realisation that these teachers were not always right? Ever thought, *something just doesn't sit right with me about this?* When do you start thinking for yourself and not blindly following an external so-called authority?

Research, education, discussions, conscious listening and opening your mind to innovative ideas is just the beginning. The challenge is to find the courage to say goodbye to your past and to make changes that will take you on a new path of life. Saying goodbye to that which no longer serves, frees you to trust your own guidance and intuition. It's there, we all have it. Your personal journey of discovery accelerates when you can forgive the past and find the courage to move forward in faith.

Introduction

Finding my Tribe

"What would you do if you had the time and resources to do something you've always wanted to do?" Many have asked me this in conversation. My reply has always been: "I'd like to sit quietly at my computer and write all day."

"Goodness, really?" many replied. It seemed their preferred pastimes ranged from playing golf, rescuing wild animals, visiting shopping centres, to having coffee with friends, watching movies on Netflix, painting, reading, and travelling. The options appeared endless.

Such ambition! I personally hadn't thought of any of those.

"You should write a biography. God knows you've had so many difficult trials over the years," those who knew me well suggested. One friend, obviously bored with my regular rants, suggested I write a story about my daughter Alice, as she IS my life, implying I had no other challenging experiences worth documenting.

Write my memoirs! How many times have I heard that idea?

But where do I begin? Do I have the appropriate writing skills to eloquently describe a candid snapshot of my life's journey? Goodness, if it's going to be a tell-all, I'll be divulging many very unflattering and even embarrassing experiences along the way. Will I be making a complete fool of myself for the sake of fulfilling a writing ambition?

Doubts! Doubts, and more doubts! A feeling, I'm sure, experienced by all who ever had the same ludicrous idea of wanting to write their own story.

I know, I'll join a writing group.

Internet research led me to attend a meeting at Scribblers Mandurah Murray Writing Group, where I was welcomed by the devilish Val, a gregarious woman of senior years. My newfound friend introduced me to members of the group, many of whom were published authors, acclaimed poets, and/or award-winning writers. I was in complete awe and felt totally out of my depth.

Every meeting involved a literary presentation, an impromptu writing exercise and a homework reading segment. At the conclusion of each session, a weekly assignment was set. As their latest writer-wannabee, the excitement grew within my being. Blind Freddie could have detected my overwhelming display of enthusiasm as I embraced every single assignment, every writing exercise, and every opportunity to refine my new craft.

"Don't forget the Five Plot Points," instructed Christine, aka C.M. Elliott, published author, teacher extraordinaire, and much respected member of the group. "In your writing you must include inciting moments, surprises, things should get worse. The goal posts must be changed, the odds increased, the protagonist must feel like she is up a tree, and the antagonists keep throwing rocks at her. Let it get worse before it gets better. Include twists and turns, selfish traits, even make the reader think *serves her right*, show emotion, give action, make the reader shudder, laugh, and cry." The final command being, "Show, don't tell, referring to the use of dialogue to engage the reader. Then wrap it up. Don't loiter."

Yay, I can do this, I will do this, I vowed deep within.

Then she went on to enlighten us about getting one's work beta-read (test read), edited, and proofread. Luckily, she had me champing at the bit when she discussed the five-plot points, as I'm sure I didn't hear a word about the lengths one must go to source a publisher. I didn't hear the bit about rejection, resilience, or persistence. Not a word! Just as well or perhaps I may have given up there and then.

However, as with membership to any group with which I have ever been associated, came a personal commitment and responsibility to its members. I soon learned it was not for me to just take from these remarkable, learned people. I also had to be prepared to give back. Within two months of joining Scribblers, I was elected Secretary, unopposed. I wondered if they saw me coming. *I must stop showing my exuberance!* At the time of writing this chapter, I was in my second term in that role.

Once again, I embraced the position, and chose to write weekly newsletters for the members' benefit. I enthusiastically complete all set assignments and, time permitting, revisited my memoir.

Nevertheless, I found myself in stimulating company. Writing disciplines were adopted, knowledge and expertise gained. I set myself the achievable task of writing at least two thousand words a week. My peers offered to critique my work, mentor me, give encouragement, and

answer my literary queries. And most importantly: rewarding relationships, even firm friendships were formed.

I set about pursuing my writing dream. With each chapter, I re-
lived the emotions of my past as I related the good, the bad and the
ugly. I wrote and wrote. It was as though each of the keys on my laptop
functioned automatically. In solitude, I pounded away week after week,
month after month. Words added, words deleted, synonyms sourced.
Conjunctive words in, prepositions out, punctuation reviewed. Friends
proof reading, peers correcting.

Fifty separate stories were written. Many about me, two about my
husband Ray, several: my parents, Anna, and Harald and a few: my
children, Glen, Erica, and Alice. These stories were all not written in
chronological order but do reflect a common theme: With Every Goodbye, you learn.

Thank you, Scribblers, I discovered my passion and, in the process,
found my tribe.

***

"How's the book coming along?" many have since asked. Well,
isn't that the problem? I've brazenly spouted my writing ambition to
friends and family, and have left them waiting, not necessarily patiently, for tangible evidence of my self-professed literary talent. With my
own pre-published hype, they want to see, not necessarily read, a shiny
professionally bound novel with my name shamelessly displayed on
its cover.

All I can say is "It won't happen overnight, but it will happen!"
Life does have a habit of getting in the way of my best laid plans.

***

Now that's enough talking. Let's get on with my story.

Chapter 1

With Every Goodbye, You'll Learn

I imagine the preliminaries to my current incarnation to have been something like this:

"Okay, have I got an assignment for you!" instructed my guiding spirit, as he woke me from my peaceful, heavenly slumber.

"Now?" I asked.

"There's a young couple down there, Anna and Harald, and they are soon to conceive a baby, and that's where you come into it," he explained as he pointed them out.

"Wow, I can see Ingelheim, Germany (West Germany at that time). Oh, the Rhineland has the most beautiful scenery, will I be living there?"

"No," he laughed.

"Now I see Hamburg. That port city is so old and gloomy, and the town is in ruins. I can't see myself living among the devastation of the second world war," I gasped.

"You won't be, but you will be conceived there. Your father will refuse to raise you in a city full of destruction, cruel memories, cramped living conditions with limited employment opportunities. Harald, being an impulsive man, will shock his entire family, including your mother Anna, and will arrange for her, your sisters Imtraud-Anna and Gabriela, and himself to emigrate to Australia."

"Australia! Is that beautiful like Germany?"

"Nothing like it! You will end up in a remote, arid, wheat farming region in the mid-west of Western Australia, where your dad will find work as a farmhand. Initially, neither he nor your mother will be able to speak English, but they will eventually master the language. This new life will be especially hard on your mother who, although robust in body and gentle in spirit, will still be fragile in mind, as she grieves her own horrific war time experiences, the early loss of her own girlhood, and the premature death of her father. She will always have the feeling of having been wrenched away from her mother and six younger siblings, several of whom she helped bring into the world. She will leave her beautiful homeland, something she will never come to terms with. However, as a loyal wife of the fifties, Anna will be obedient to her husband.

As post World War II German migrants in that harsh new country, your parents will face many hardships including ignorance and prejudice. Due to the locals' lack of knowledge, your parents will be blamed for the atrocities of Hitler's regime and will often be made to feel like outcasts. However, working as a family unit, they will succeed as they set about making a comfortable life for themselves and their three daughters. Their special attributes will be hard work, resilience, tenacity, mountains of determination, plus an ingrained faith in their creator.

"Goodness, couldn't you get something easier for me?"

"You don't do easy! Anyone can do *easy*! You personally will thrive on challenge as you'll learn the meaning of peace, forgiveness, and wisdom, and believe me, you'll need every single one of these as you search for your place in the world. So, watch, listen and learn," he added.

"Will it be difficult for me?"

"Difficult, but not impossible! Your childhood will be your classroom, as you learn the art of hard physical work as you toil in your parents' business. However, eventually, you'll find the discipline in everything you undertake, and will experience pride in your achievements. You'll learn resilience and the importance of being a stayer and not a quitter, as you search for your own place and identity.

At an early age, you will give birth to a son who will always be the apple of your eye. He will have inherited learning issues, but will surprise everyone with his strong work ethic, his gregarious disposition, his own special determination, and his entrepreneurial skills.

Two years later, you will give birth to a daughter, and let me tell you now, you had better hold on to your hat, as she will take you on a very merry ride. Energy will abound in this blond-haired bombshell! She'll be noisy, fun loving, exuberant, active and will always be a blessing to you. She'll be an independent soul, so let her go and let her be, we'll take it from there.

Oh, now here's the hard bit. Eight years after her birth, you will feel a sudden gush of maternal instinct. Immediately, you will fall pregnant with another daughter. She will choose you as her mother. This special child will be sent from heaven above, to shape you into the person we have sent you to become. Expect the unexpected! She will refuse to be trained in the futility of your world, and her thinking will be contrary to your way of thinking. She will challenge your every word, your every belief, and your every choice. Although she will reject your affections, she'll need large doses of unconditional love, patience, forgiveness, and mostly, your presence. Yes, she will test you to the edge of your limits."

"Will she have any good traits?" I begged the question.

"Yes, she will be creative, have a love of music (her music, not yours), and animals. She will have an affinity with nature, so get ready as she fights to save the whales, free the bears, rescue the orangutans, and takes in stray cats. She may even want to dig up your exotic garden to plant vegetables."

"I'm not sure that I'm up for this assignment. Will I have any support?"

"Your guides will be by your side the entire time to help share the load. I'll also station an angel at every crossroad to give further directions, so listen hard. But fear not, I'll be with you, and remember, with every goodbye, you'll learn! This is the assignment if you care to accept it."

With the above information encrypted into my DNA, but not in my memory, my spirit commenced its bodily journey at the Merredin District Hospital on the 22nd of January 1954. On this day Anna printed my name, Karin Lorek, in her little red birthday book, next to the date and this text:

> *You are self-reliant, diplomatic, fond of dressing well and care a great deal for the good opinion of your friends and business associates. Secretive, but not to the extent of trickery. You are affectionate, and lovable and should make a happy circle wherever you are.*

Chapter 2

My Father: The Thinker

Harald, the first born,18th November 1929, to a family of seven children, living in cramped conditions in the Port City of Hamburg, West Germany, became fiercely self-reliant. A dreamer with a zest for life who vowed to never waste a moment of it.

And he didn't! With his own self determined blueprint for life, as a young man he bided his time, learning new skills, making his own judgements, strategically planning, setting a path of preparation for his life's adventure, and living that dream without fear or favour from his parents, his siblings, or his countrymen.

The Lorek family lived in Wilhelmsburg, a housing estate located on the outskirts of Hamburg. It was an area which prided itself on its 19th century architecture, adjacent green fields, and its proximity to the Hamburg Port, the second largest port in the world, situated on the banks of the Elbe River.

Harald's early years saw him playing in the neighbouring fields with his sister Gerda, as they stalked wild deer, chased school friends, and gathered berries from low bushes, before returning home to his loving mother and his strict yet hard-working father.

He was eleven when the Second World War broke out. These times brought food shortages as crops and fresh food were commandeered by the government to feed the German troops. The people had added fears, not only of the enemy bombs, but also of their own government and their freedom of individualism and beliefs. Internal movement was denied without the appropriate authority. Hate propaganda in relation to the enemy: the Russians, the Americans, their fellow Jewish citizens, and people of colour, was constantly broadcast. Loathing of these enemies was mandated and failure to display agreement led to instant incarceration and/or death. Consequently, thousands of compassionate German citizens disappeared from the streets and were never heard from again.

In his adolescent years, Harald and his sisters would climb buildings to gain a view of the spectacular fire shows: the enemy air raids on Hamburg City. He witnessed the city's desecration and destruction. He watched-on from a distance as phosphorous bombs were being indiscriminately dropped on housing estates. He saw burning, contaminated people running from buildings to their slow, excruciatingly painful death. He described this sight as watching huge fireflies swarming and then, suddenly, the lights would disappear.

Harald, too young for army conscription, was ordered to leave school at the age of 13, to work on a Nazi farm. That farm had been requisitioned by the government to be a prime food source for German soldiers, the landowner being rewarded with an SS Officer ranking due to his obedience. Harald's parents, Edmund and Martha, like most of the working-class, were living in poverty, and had become disillusioned with the promises of the Nazi regime. However, the people were forced to conform. Everyone knew that nonconformity meant death. When Harald managed to sneak farm fresh vegetables back to his hungry family on his weekends off, his father angrily threw the Nazi produce out, refusing to have anything to do with the farm or reigning government.

At this point, I'm sure you're wondering why my family's Nazi past is being glossed over.

My mother's father and five of my uncles were conscripted (forcibly taken in the dark of night) into the German army when the second world war broke out. Does that make them 'the Nazis,' who our English textbooks describe as the most despicable people on Earth? German men, following orders from their powerful leader, were fighting to protect their homeland. They followed Hitler because he promised an improved, richer Germany. Once that groundswell for a better homeland gathered momentum, the people were trapped by that leader, and were forced to conform. Nonconformity meant death!

I travelled to Germany for the specific task of researching this book. I walked the childhood paths of my parents. I visited their schools, shops, rivers, hills, playgrounds, bunkers, air raid shelters, and war time ruins in Hamburg and Ingelheim. I visited the Sachsenhausen concentration camp, 34 kilometres from Berlin, and the Jewish Holocaust Memorial in Berlin. Was I repulsed by German history? Yes, I was. Am I also repulsed by English and Australian history? Yes, I am.

***

At the end of the war in 1945, destitute, displaced families followed the masses, all waiting for leadership from a fallen government in a defeated war-torn country. They were waiting for someone or something to show them the way to a better future. Waiting, complaining, hungry, homelessness: such words were not in the realms of Harald's thinking. At 16, he had already seen more than his fair share of sickening violence, sheer misery, and death. What he wanted was hope, lifestyle prospects, to be able to provide for a future wife and family, and he wanted it now. *Now* being the operative word. His nature was to think for himself, to create opportunities for himself and to strive to achieve the ideals of his own reality.

When offered a secure-for-life position as a ships carpenter at the neighbouring docks, to follow in his father's footsteps, to re-live his father's life, Harald saw it only as temporary, a means to provide funds for his own education. His love for the land, presented to him during those war years, gave him a dream to become a farmer. He set about enrolling at the Hamburg Agricultural College to further his education. Working at the docks by day, and studying at night, set him on his chosen path.

Ingelheim, am Rhine, the centre of the wine-growing region of West Germany, is the town where he met and fell in love with Anna Schwarz while on secondment to study viticulture, a division of his agricultural course. As was Harald's nature, he didn't let the grass grow under his feet or let the grapes rot on the vines, as they say. Before long they had a child on the way and were married. He was 21 years of age and Anna was 19.

Back in Hamburg, accommodation was scarce, so there was no choice but to move in with his parents, Edmund and Martha, in their small, rented, three-bedroom apartment. Conditions were cramped and not ideal, especially when the second child, a daughter, Gabriela, followed two years, almost to the day from the birth of their first daughter, Imtraud Anna. *What is happening to me? This is not what I want for myself or for my family. I want so much more than this*, he thought. *When I finish my agriculture degree, I will make radical changes.*

On graduation, just five months after Gabriela's birth, he learned his wife Anna was again pregnant. Great despair overwhelmed him. That's when he saw a poster on the school's pin-up board: "Farmers Wanted in Australia." *Well, that's good enough for me, that's the sign*

I've been waiting for, he strongly believed, and went straight into the Immigration Department to apply for passage for his family of four to travel to Australia on a work visa.

Due to his Agricultural degree, Harald had been assured a job in Kununurra, a newly developed area in the far north of Western Australia. The Western Australian Government was building its channel irrigation system with a view to growing fruit and vegetables. His skills were required to pilot that project.

Australia: he hadn't heard much about that far flung country. He didn't know north, south, east, or west but he did know the proposition sounded too good to pass over. To be eligible for this scheme, he must work in Australia for a period of two years. After that time, he could return to Germany or apply for Australian citizenship, should the family choose to stay.

The Hamburg Lorek family were not impressed with their eldest son. He was leaving his homeland to go and find a life of his own choosing in some far-flung foreign land. A place none of them knew anything about.

"That's Harald, he's so impatient. If he will just wait a few more years, Hamburg will be rebuilt and there'll be houses and jobs for everyone. He is a fool!" they said, and refused to wave farewell to the young family as they boarded the train to Bremerhaven where they were to take the passenger ship to Australia.

Goodbye my homeland. Auf wiedersehen meine heimat!

***

A gruelling three-week boat trip followed as the family shared small spaces with hundreds of other European immigrants. The journey was particularly uncomfortable for two-month pregnant Anna as she experienced chronic morning sickness, plus cared for the active seven-month-old and the clingy two-year-old. Harald enjoyed the trip. Wherever he went, he carried his wooden chess set, crafted by his father's own hands, and always managed to find a willing partner. The game of chess, a skill taught to him by his father, became his life-long passion. Time would fly as he pursued opponent after opponent: his clear thinking and his ability to strategize, prepared him for his life ahead.

On arrival at Fremantle on 9th July 1953, Harald was greeted by an official from the Agricultural Board of WA and flown directly to Kununurra. Meanwhile Anna and the girls were bussed one hundred kilometres inland from Perth to Northam Holden Camp, a primitive migrant institution. So typical of its time, the camp consisted of groups of Nissen huts, semi cylindrical sheet metal huts built around a large common use facility.

His time in Kununurra was short lived, as on his arrival, he learned his promised family house had not been built and it could be over a year before he would be reunited with Anna and the girls. Harald, frustrated and disappointed, left the far north of Western Australia after just three weeks and re-joined his wife and daughters at the Northam Camp.

Camp life was centred around learning to speak English and finding a job. At the time, farmers from far away farming areas drove to the camp to recruit farm labourers. Mr Reichelt, a third-generation German farmer, whose family had years before headed west from South Australia to take up farming at Korbel, travelled the 160 kilometres to the camp searching for a farmhand. Harald quickly volunteered for the position and was soon waving farewell, from the back of the farmer's utility to his wife, yet again. He was assured accommodation, but would first need to fix it up, as it was currently being used as shearers' quarters. Harald had no idea where he was being taken. Anna had no idea where he was going, nor when he would be back to collect her. There were few phones in this remote place. She busied herself caring for the girls and fulfilling her part of the New Australian's bargain; learning to speak English.

"*Zis iss a cup. Zat iss a dok (dog). My name iss Anna," she would repeatedly say. "Tank you. Jou're velcome," phrases which were to irk her until her passing.

In the meantime, Harald was working on a wheat and sheep farm. How amazing it was for him to see such vast expanses of land, massive flocks of sheep and so much different, and larger, machinery. He was free at last. Each day was a learning curve, a new experience and, in the process, he was learning to speak English as there was no one around who could speak German.

True to his word, three months later, Harald returned to Holden Camp, driving the farm utility, to collect his now heavily pregnant wife and two young daughters. The promised house was basic, shabby, and small, so Anna set about making their first marital home cosy and comfortable for the family.

Harald was living the dream, away from his narrow-thinking family of origin, with new challenges and lessons every day. He met and drank beer with neighbouring farmers and learned of their visions and aspirations. He played chess on his day-off and was able to take his family to the Lutheran Church in Merredin on Sundays, where he would meet up with several other second and third-generation German families. He was being very well cared for by his wife. His children, Anne, Gaby (names now abbreviated to make pronunciation easier for locals) and third daughter, Karin, were well trained, well behaved and woe betide if they ever put a foot out of line!

Once the two-year probationary period was up, Harald and Anna revoked their option to return to Germany and, several years later, went on to become Australian citizens.

*In German, TH is pronounced like T, so having the softer H sound on the end made pronunciation difficult. Other letters the trained German tongue find nigh impossible to pronounce are: R, for example - rabbit was pronounced "hrabbit." Ray is pronounced as "Hray." G is pronounced as K; D as T; V as W; W as V; J as Y, and Y as J (Jarvis became Yarwis) and so on. In later years, my husband's name was to cause great tongue twisting difficulty and mirth among my German relatives as they each tried unsuccessfully to say his name. So confusing for German students of English, and perhaps painful to listen to by those schooled in perfect English.

Chapter 3

My Mother: The Support Act

Anna was born to parents Margaritha and Fredrich Schwarz on a chilly winter day on 14th December 1932 in Ingelheim, West Germany. For those who aren't familiar with the geography of Germany, Ingelheim is an historic village on the banks of the river Rhine, approximately 50 kilometres from the city of Frankfurt. The area is famous for the ruins of the 16th Century Castle of Karl the Great and Pierrot Wines. The village is celebrated as being Die Rotweinstadt (The Red Wine Town) where a wine festival is held annually. Today its major industry is Boehringer Pharmaceuticals, makers of Alka-Seltzer and other must-have drugs.

Anna's family home was a primitive house of stone, built against the ruins of Karl the Great's Castle. Today that house, fully restored, is a tourist attraction. There she lived her entire young life as the eldest of the Schwartz brood of seven children, and periodically with her half-sister and half-brother, born to her mother in a previous marriage.

As was so typical of the times, the eldest child had much responsibility and Anna was called upon to care for her younger siblings as they, one by one, entered the world. Cooking, cleaning, sewing, and child minding was the order of the day. Not playing, laughing, reading or just being a kid. Responsibility, hard work, and sacrifice were imposed on her from an incredibly early age, and this was the path she continued to walk for the rest of her life.

Anna loved her beautiful Ingelheim: to go to the fields to pick fresh produce, walk along the high banks of the scenic Rhine River, skip along the cobble-stone pavers to the markets, explore the neighbouring ruins, meet with the villagers for chats, and attend the local school to see her friends. This was Anna's Ingelheim, and she loved it so.

Anna was eight years old when World War II broke out. However, this was not a war that was battled in some far away country, this war was fought in and around Anna's Ingelheim. Her domestic responsibilities grew, when her much loved father and uncles were conscripted, and sent off to fight a war about which they knew nothing. Life was hard for the villagers. The fresh produce from the fields was commandeered to feed the German soldiers, leaving little for the villagers to exchange with their meagre allocated coupons.

For almost six years the Rhineland skies, streets, hills, and waterways became a battlefield before her very eyes. Regular bombings, desecration, ruination, bloodied roads, dead bodies at every turn, occupation of forceful soldiers amidst the piercing sounds of men yelling, women screaming, and air raid sirens blaring in the background, all a part of her every moment. Being frozen with terror, having a hungry stomach, and fearing death were her daily realities.

Each day Anna and her mother made it a priority to keep the little children safe, clean and fed. Anna often sacrificed her own safety, her own food allocations, and her own childhood to put that family first.

In 1945 the war ended. Her father returned home. Anna was fifteen years old and as the months went by, she was handed two more little sisters, eighteen months apart, to care for.

Sadly, her father had contracted an illness during the war, and she watched-on in grief as he slowly died. Heartbroken, as she had adored her Papa, Anna once again assumed the role of an adult. She was now old enough to go out and earn a wage to help support the family. Some of the town's wealthier people employed her to cook, clean, sew, and polish floors for them. Each week her meagre wage would go directly into her mother's hand to pay the household expenses. Anna always did what she did so well, and that was work!

From time to time, she would escape up to the Waldeck, her favourite special high spot overlooking the village: rows of vineyards, the river Rhine, and the scenic Rhine Valley. Here she would just sit, rest, and enjoy her Ingelheim. One day in 1949, in one of her stolen moments on the hillside, a young man came riding along on his bike and saw her sitting there.

He stopped. Their eyes met. He was tall, dark, and totally handsome. He rode off. Anna felt her heart skip a beat. Before long, she looked up and saw the young man had come cycling back towards her and stopped directly in front of her.

"Hello, my name is Harald," he said.

They chatted. Before long, he walked with her down the hillside to her humble home. Harald made her feel so special, but she cautiously believed this young man was too good to be true. She slowly started to play hard to get, as she didn't think this handsome man could really be interested in her. But that young man, persistent in his desires, kept up his visits, and soon became a regular at her family home.

However, Harald, an agriculture student from Hamburg, was only visiting Ingelheim as part of his studies of grape vines and would shortly be returning to Hamburg to complete his agriculture degree. When the day came for Harald to leave, Anna felt so sick. The love of her life was leaving. She became sicker by the day. Then even sicker! Why did she feel so sick?

Uh oh! Anna was with child. However, in her usual self-sacrificing nature, she didn't wish to ruin Harald's chances of success, so she made it her business to not tell him of his impending fatherhood. On 5th November 1950, Anna gave birth to Imtraud Anna in the same house where she herself was born. She didn't tell Harald, as she didn't want to burden him. He was ambitious. He had a bright future ahead of him.

Thankfully, Anna's mother intervened and wrote a letter to Harald, telling him the news.

Nervous, excited, and frantic, Harald hurriedly made his way back to Ingelheim to meet his little daughter, and on 10th March 1951, Anna and Harald were married.

***

Korbel, Western Australia, January 1954. Anna felt the familiar pains of contractions grip her body and knew her third child was about to make its appearance. Harald quickly brought out the farm truck, helped Anna aboard, and drove along the washed-out gravel track for fifteen kilometres to the nearby town of Merredin to drop her off at the hospital.

"Right, must get back, I'll see you in a few days," he said.

Fortunately for Anna, she had befriended the mother of the farm owner who assisted with the care of the little Anne and Gaby. Anna was alone in childbirth. She had only a limited smattering of the English language, but like the brave woman she had always had to be, Anna delivered baby Karin into the world on January 22nd.

Country farm life became the family's lifestyle for the next three years. Anna cared for her husband, three daughters, cooked for the shearers, attended the Country Women's Association, sewed clothing for her girls, sent little Anne to school on the school bus, and attended the Lutheran Church in Merredin on Sundays. These times were particularly tough for Anna, who, although strong in body was totally capable of doing anything she set her mind to. But she still carried the mental scars of her past and did not adapt easily to the social setting of her new frontier environment. Her only social outlet was to meet with farmers' wives, the landed gentry of the day, who would become impatient with her broken-English, blame her for Germany's war history and would question this foreign family's right to live in their exclusive country. Ignorance played a part in their prejudices, and Anna would become very emotionally sensitive as she felt them sniggering and judging behind her back.

The years that followed saw Anna and Harald move into the Merredin township, where they set about planning their first home of their very own. Harald, working as a builder's labourer, and Anna, working in a restaurant, managed to save sufficient money to buy a half-acre block of land. Harald initially built a two-room shed where the family lived, while he built their modern spacious asbestos and tile three-bedroom house. On completion of the new house at 5 Colin Street Merredin, Anna used her homemaking skills to create a beautiful home for her family.

During this time, several special local families gave their support to this new Australian family, and the young girls quickly adopted themselves an Aunty Lisa, an Uncle Kasey, a godmother Rita, a Grandma Reichelt, Mummy and Daddy Ivy, and a cousin Ronald.

In 1961, Anna became pregnant again and for the first time, enjoyed the pregnancy. She had a lovely home, had decorated a room for the baby, and had knitted dozens of tiny garments as she awaited the birth. Harald was secretly hoping for a son, as with three daughters, he was feeling outnumbered. At the time of her admission to hospital for the birth, my sisters and I were staying with Aunty Lisa, and I remember, like yesterday, Dad saying:

"The baby boy has died."

As it happened, Mum had a small pelvis, and the baby weighed twelve pounds at birth. The Doctor at the time saw fit to leave her in labour for three days before performing a botched caesarean section. The baby, named Terrance Harald, had suffered severe head injuries during the birth and, I suspect, was left to die a natural death in the linen room.

Dad, unsure of how to react, played the stoic husband and provider. He insisted that Mum be grateful for the three daughters she had at home. Before Anna was even discharged from hospital, Dad had arranged for the baby to be buried at the local cemetery. No funeral. Just Dad, the pastor, and the grave digger.

Anna tried to be brave, but in her weaker moments, would curl up on her bed and cry her heart out. Grieving was not permitted in our household. We were all to be strong and go forward. I'm sure it didn't help either when we girls excitedly asked:

"Can we have the baby clothes you made, for our dolls?

My mother never got over the death of her son, not even in her later years.

Chapter 4

Cinderella

"No mummy, nooo," I screamed. "I'm sorry. I didn't mean to do it. I'm sorry! I'm sorry!

Once again, I wasn't even sure what I was apologising for. Was it because I had accidentally broken the switch on the Mixmaster as I was cleaning it? Was it because I mentioned I didn't like the oxtail stew she had prepared for dinner? Was it because I had inadvertently allowed the potatoes to burn in the pot? Misdemeanour, accident, faux pas, a thrashing was warranted, and we all knew Mummy would feel so much better in herself after she had done that which needed to be done. She had told me often enough that I was an ungrateful, dumb, useless, and lazy. I apparently deserved a good hiding.

Unresolved emotions from her scarred past plagued my mother's mind for her entire adult life. My father had certainly got the best deal in the relationship. He was fun loving, intelligent and socially accepted in the community. Mum, however, other than trying to satisfy Dad's needs, and keeping an immaculate home, had no interests of her own. She'd jealously watch-on as her handsome, popular husband was living his dream.

On this day, like most other days, she was tired. She had been up since 5.30am and had been working in their commercial laundry business where she'd stood ironing dozens and dozens of white starched business shirts and damask tablecloths by hand for the town's wealthiest people. By 5pm her workday was done, and she could then attend to her family's needs, but woe betide if anything was out of place when she walked through the door to our home. My sisters and I would keep an eye and an ear out for her arrival, each of us hoping we had covered every base. We'd always tried to ensure the house was clean, the potatoes were on to boil, the table was set for dinner and there was nothing out of place that could irritate her. One small hint of annoyance, and the nearest daughter to the action would cop a beating.

That night, it was my turn, but I was never ever sure why. Without warning, I felt mum's strong hand slap against my mouth. A sharp pain startled me, as my teeth pierced my lips. Numbness and blood followed. I fell backwards to the floor. Mum pounced over me like a tiger on its prey and began to smash her robust, bare hands around my head and to any part of my body I wasn't quick enough to pull out of the line of attack. The resentments of a lifetime, festering within, yet never far from the surface, spewed forth in an eruption of volcanic proportions.

Her soft, white face turned red with rage. Her eyes, contorted into small slits, reflected her revulsion for me. She was like a deranged madwoman out of control. I cowered on the floor and covered my head with my arms to protect myself from the next blow. I attempted to scream out for her to stop, but all that came out of my mouth was saliva, blood, and a muffled gurgling sound. Just momentarily, I used a hand to wipe the concoction of tears and mucus from my face. I felt another excruciating blow to my head. I heard a roar, as blood rushed to my brain.

"I'm sorry Mummy, I'm sorry!"

Every hit smashed into my young flesh. Pent-up rage had overtaken her mind, and I knew she wouldn't stop pounding until every ounce of raw emotion had been drained from her tired, overworked body. Even at such an early age, I had taught myself to disconnect my mind from my physical self and imagine I was an onlooker to this horrific scene. I saw myself rolling with the punches, writhing, bleeding, and sobbing as red, hand-shaped welts appeared on exposed areas of my body. In my mind's eye, I saw myself in my happy place, at the ball, where I danced with Prince Charming. I wore a beautiful white ball-gown. The prince fell in love with me and whisked me away on his white horse and we lived happily ever after.

Back to reality. If I just whimpered in a repentant manner and kept apologising, perhaps Mummy would see that I was truly sorry, would feel better, and calm down.

"I'm sorry Mummy, I'm sorry!"

Once her anger had subsided, she stepped back, clearly shaken, and began to massage her now bruised and swollen ironing hand. She then fumbled into her handbag for a bottle of Dolamins, an anti-inflammatory drug with analgesic properties. Without counting, she poured a small heap of white tablets onto the palm of her hand and threw them down her neck like a pro. No water, no coffee. She'd done that before on so many occasions. Dolomins, it seemed, was the *go-to* elixir for everything, and always took pride of place at the top of her weekly shopping list.

"Now get up and do some work. And if you don't shut up, I'll give you something else to cry about," she spat.

Shaking, panting, and struggling to breathe, I grabbed a broom and began to sweep the floor, not that it was dirty. My sisters and I had seen to that earlier on, but at least I was working. I was doing something!

My mind was anaesthetised, my body trembled, my heart ached for love and my spirit had died, yet again.

Prince Charming, where are you now? I cried out under my breath.

***

My mother had a reactive nature, a trait learned from her own mother, and a mothering style she handed down to her own daughters. She became angry when tired, was not in control of a situation or felt helpless. When words of anger did not suffice, she'd resort to physical abuse to make her point. She'd continue until her nervous system was relieved and she was physically exhausted.

Mum's volatility took its toll on her three daughters. My sisters have their own account of their reactions, but that is their story. I developed a fear of not pleasing my parents or those in authority. I became a people pleaser. I feared not being good enough for my parents' love, for God's love or for anyone's love. I believed I had to earn love by going over and beyond with honourable deeds, creative initiatives, unquestionable obedience, and sheer hard work. I needed to have my happy, helpful public persona on display to achieve the rewards I sought. I believed the teaching of my childhood to be absolute. I felt powerless to think for myself. I became intolerant to laziness, weakness, and ignorance. *Can't they see? Don't they know? Didn't they learn?* I became judgemental and saw the same flaws in others that I tried to hide in myself. I was my own harshest critic. Striving for perfection became my life's mission.

This darker side of my mother I have forgiven, and today choose not to focus upon. Mum had vivid war time experiences, which I have mentioned. She had been severely mentally damaged in her younger years, and I came to understand that *hurt people, hurt people*. My heart has always gone out to her. I understand why she couldn't enjoy life to the fullest: countless painful memories, and nowhere to go for help or healing. In so many ways, she was a thoughtful and loving person. Each one of her grandchildren and great grandchildren adored her and will be quite shocked to read my depiction of these childhood memories. I have illustrated her generous and caring traits in the chapter entitled *Auf Wiedersehen Anna.*

Chapter 5

Young Ray (Scoe) Jarvis

Oh, bugger, there's the school bus, lamented 12-year-old Ray, aka Scoe, as he prepared to scramble aboard. He, his two older brothers, and his three sisters lined up for it every day of their school lives. How he dreaded seeing that big orange beast as it came rolling down the hill towards his road-side bus-stop. *A few more years of this waste of time and I will be able to leave that place and work on the farm. Heaps better than school.*

Ray displayed his love for all things West Perth Football Club by wearing club colours as much as possible, even taking his nickname Scoe from a West Perth Football Club player great, Ray Schofield. Dressed in school attire of choice, a red football jumper with a wide dark blue diagonal stripe, and ill-fitting hand-me-down grey shorts, he would often stoop to pick up a few gravel stones for a last-minute throw. He'd aim at his target, the Merredin Town sign, one hundred metres further down the road. *Yay. Bullseye!* That was his *dead-eye-dick* fast bowling practice for the day.

He'd grab his small, tattered leather satchel, fling it across one shoulder before clambering aboard, ensuring he didn't mess his dad-cut, sandy blond hair, which each morning he'd set in place with generous lashings of Californian Poppy hair oil. The satchel was used just for carrying his lunch, as he would jest, for as sure as heck there'd be no homework or even a book ever to be found in there.

Oops, my footy, I forgot my footy. It's bad enough going to school, let alone without a footy. Darn!

It was standing room only on the Nukarni Bus, the circle route taken to collect the farm kids from northern outlying areas. The Jarvis stop was the last pick-up for the morning and the first drop-off in the afternoon. Their farm, being metres from the town boundary, although just two kilometres from the North Merredin Primary School's door-step, still qualified the family for free school transport. Ray would stand with his nose to the side window, facing his farm to check if there was anything happening that he might be missing out on. Some days he'd hear his father, Charlie, firing up a tractor and would know by the noise it made if it was the International, the Deutz or the Chamberlain. Often, he'd see his dad driving off in the truck and would know exactly where he was going and for what reason.

He'd note the black cockatoos as they landed in the paddock and knew the rains were coming. He knew the meaning of each cloud and what impact they would have on the success of the year's wheat crop. At shearing time, he would see the sheep being drafted into pens over at the shearing shed. He felt robbed because he was not allowed to stay home to help the shearers with wool classing, wool pressing, or branding the newly shorn sheep.

He'd see his mother, Myra, feeding the chooks and ducks and wonder if she'd find any newborn ducklings or chickens in the wood heap that day. He'd see a mother cat and her kittens gathering around the milk trough filled with the freshly squeezed offering of Molly, the Red Poll home cow. He wondered if there'd be plentiful milk left in the bucket for his mum to make separated cream or would there be just enough to boil up for scalded cream. Either way, yum!

"Mooooooo!" he'd yell out through the open bus window to Molly as they drove past her paddock. Molly always looked up and moo-d back. Ray would laugh with so much joy. *Must tell Dad there is a loose wire at the end of the cow paddock. I don't want Molly to get her leg stuck in that.* Ray always stored important farm information in his head. He loved the farm he was born to. He loved the array of garages, one for his dad's car and one for his mum's, the corrugated iron sheds, some hoarding a treasure trove of paraphernalia from the horse and cart days. Another housed breeding pigs, and two large sheds stored stacks of dry hay. There was a milking shed, a horse stable, a lean-to for the new Claas Header, a repurposed army shed which had been transported to the property to house the trotting horses' paraphernalia. There was another shed for sundries which Dad had proudly purchased for a pittance at clearing sales. There were shelters for the machinery: the combines (seeding machine), the scarifiers (soil tilling implements), and the two farm trucks. Midday sheds, Ray would jokingly call them, because the only time these machines would have one hundred percent shade, would be at midday. Tall shiny metal wheat and barley silos added height and contrast to the landscape of buildings.

Tucked away in the front corner of the ever-expanding farmyard was the original weatherboard farmhouse, built in the 1920s, now dilapidated, but still used for storing old bits and pieces that might come in handy one day.

Nearby stood a 1960s style, four-bedroom, green painted asbestos house, with a long sleep-out across the back veranda: his bedroom. To those passing by, the Jarvis farm appeared like a thriving village.

Arriving at school, Ray would spring off the bus, race to his classroom, hang his satchel on the pegs provided, and race off to find his mates to have a kick of the footy before school. *Best part of school*, he thought. However, that's where the fun ended. Once the old school bell rang, his heart would sink. *Oh no!* As the second youngest of six children, Ray had already learnt to play the survival game, when to project his desires, when to pick his fights and when to let the ball go through to the keeper. *If I stay quiet, no one will notice me. Gees, I can't sit still. I think I'll sharpen my pencils. Oops, I just spilt ink everywhere. I'm in trouble again! I wish playtime would hurry up. I'm hungry already. I hope its lunch time soon. Then there'll be social studies or hopefully manual arts after play time and then I'll go home. Oh no, I must go through this same boring school stuff until I'm 15. I can't wait to leave school and work on the farm.*

At that time, in the 50s and 60s, students were categorised as either smart kids or as "slow learners." Ray, due to his undiagnosed dyslexia and dysgraphia, was in the latter group. The teachers would openly show favour towards the clever children while the "dumb ones" were left to fend for themselves. Often, these children were labelled as delinquent, class clowns or dunces, and were daily thrown out of class for being disruptive. Consequently, a gold star, a pat on the back, teacher's pet, a class acting or singing opportunity, or even a word of encouragement was never afforded Ray. Did he care? No!

"Just get me through the next few years because I'm leaving school anyway," he'd say.

"What do you like best about school?" Many of his mother's friends would politely ask.

"Play time, sport and home time, oh and lunch time if my sisters pack an extra piece of cake for me," he'd quickly chirp, without feeling he had to further explain himself.

Ray did, however, get his moment in the sun at school, as the sports teacher always selected him to play on the school football and cricket teams. Sport was his passion, and in this, he excelled. Through sport, Ray was able to display his true traits: his good, his bad, and his ugly side. His tenacity as a footballer to get that ball, or his wicked smarts and determination as a cricketing fast bowler to get a wicket, brought him fame among his teammates, and infamy amongst his opponents. His family and friends named him Scoe, a true sporting name. He had plenty of practice at football and cricket. With older brothers as teammates and a farm for a playground, there were always opportunities for him to enjoy these his favourite sports.

At 3.30pm every school day, the bus would drop the Jarvis kids off at their farm gate. Ray would run, not walk, up to the house, change into his farm clothes, grab a vegemite sandwich from the kitchen, and would disappear over to the farmyard to commence his round of evening chores, of which there were many. The life of a farm kid was not easy, but young Scoe could not have imagined life any other way. Work was what you did, not something to be avoided or complained about.

"The jobs weren't going to do themselves, were they?" It didn't matter how hot or cold the temperature, how heavy the bale of hay, what size the Mallee root he needed to chop, how many loads of rocks he needed to pick from the newly cleared paddocks, or how far he had to walk to herd the sheep back to their neighbouring property, Ray attacked his daily chores with gusto.

"Let's just get the job done," was his motto. If there was time after they'd finished their work, the boys would have a kick of the football, make gings (sling shots) and shoot tins off fence posts. Often, they'd build bikes out of miscellaneous scrap parts found at the town's rubbish tip. If Scoe had it his way, he would only go indoors for food and to sleep.

Indoors was where his sisters gathered as they were being groomed in the skills of housewifery. They were becoming well accomplished in the art of country women's style cooking, in cleaning up after their men folk, and sewing their own clothes. When their house chores were completed, they were then able to join the boys outside for hockey, football, skipping, and chasey if, of course, there were enough daylight hours left to enjoy.

Early each Saturday morning, rain, hail or shine, Ray would eagerly jump out of bed, complete his farm chores at record speed, and furiously pedal his home-made bike, down to the town's recreation ground to take part in a game of junior football or cricket, depending on the season. He was a real team player.

***

Thank God, I'm 15. No more pencils, no more books, no more teacher's dirty looks! Now my life can start! I need to wait another two years before I can get a driver's license, but I can already drive tractors, trucks, headers, and every other vehicle on the farm. I know how to strip down an engine, put it back together again, change tyres and fit points to a scarifier. I can weld, kill a sheep, and dress it down. I've even helped lambs be born.

In fact, there is nothing I can't do to run this place. I'm going to work on this farm forever. But I will make some changes when Dad goes. He is so old school! First thing I'll do is get rid of the cow. Gee, milking her twice a day, that's a real waste of time. You can buy milk downtown.

Another thing I won't do is build a house up here on this land when I get married. Two brothers, the old man and me, the last thing we need is another house, which I know I will have to pay for myself, on this farm. No, I think I'll buy a house in town. I've been saving for a house all my life from the money Dad gave me from collecting dead wool (wool pulled off dead rotted sheep in the paddocks).

Gee, Merredin's only a kilometre down the road. Yep, that's what I'll do. Okay, I'll keep a look out for a little house I can afford, and I'll find a nice local girl and see if she'd want to marry someone like me.

*In the meantime, I'll work here with my dad and brothers for six days of the week, and on Sundays, I'll play senior cricket for *Nokaning in the summer and league football for *Nukarni in the winter, with my brothers and my mates.*

**Nukarni: a wheat siding 20ks north of Merredin. *Nokaning: a wheat siding 10ks north of Merredin. Both were once thriving farming communities.*

Chapter 6

My Aussie Playground

Only six late fifties style homes had ever been built on this isolated, forgotten road on the outskirts of Merredin. To my sisters and me, this street was the town's best kept secret: it was our playground. As young girls, we'd scraped our knees on the corrugated gravel road, sailed our paper boats on the sheets of ochre dirt puddles, learnt to ride bikes, play tennis, skip, do cartwheels and chase each other about. Very seldom a car ventured down our way. If it did, the driver was either a neighbour or a stranger who was lost. Growing up, we'd walked this road every single day: to primary school, to high school, to the shops, to our friends' houses, and to our parents' laundry business, directly across the road, and to work. In later years, we even learnt to drive a car on this very street.

Crown land, adjacent to the laundry, had been our own bush sanctuary. As thrill seeking young girls, we spied on Aboriginal tribes as they sat around under their branch shelters. As bigger kids we made our own branch humpies, snuck cake over the road to picnic among the Wattle bushes, lit campfires, and pretended we were on a secret adventure. Very Famous Five.[1]

We'd run, yelling and screaming, waving our hands above our heads as magpies swooped during their September breeding season. We'd throw leftover crumbs at the murder of crows perched in the surrounding eucalyptus trees. We chased flocks of pink and grey galahs, green and yellow "Twenty-Eight" parrots, and watched them fly off into the clear blue sky. From time to time, we'd find kookaburras resting in one of our trees. We'd try to incite them to laugh by making our own version of kookaburra laughter sounds. Occasionally they'd delight us with a low, hiccupping chuckle, then would throw their heads back in raucous laughter. Gaby and I would join in too.

Snakes were a given in our bushland and we weren't even frightened. As we walked along the dry paths, we'd just stamp our feet to

---

[1] Blyton, Enid. *"The Famous Five,"* (A series of children's adventure books) Hodder and Stoughton. UK. 1942-62

scare them away. It was that easy! Often, we'd get our feet wedged in a rabbit burrow while exploring. Short of the odd twisted ankle, no severe damage was ever done to us, the cute little grey creatures, or their Aussie bush habitat. Walking through spider webs was child's play. We'd just take a tree branch and sweep a path for us to walk through. Somehow, without the benefit of formal environmental studies, we knew not to go anywhere near the venomous trapdoor spiders and to avoid the redback spiders.

In winter, the wild oat grasses were high enough for the Lorek girls and the neighbours' kids to play hide and seek in. In summer, the grounds were bare, brown, and appeared godforsaken. Doublegee prickles were the only source of vegetation, and how many times did we get ourselves trapped in a patch of them? Screams of pain rang throughout the neighbourhood as an ensnared kid yelled for help.

In my early teens I had kept my bay gelding, Tommy, an ex-trotting pony, in that same bushland. Nobody objected! Nobody cared!

"Tommy, you're the only one who understands me," I'd often cry into his neck as I hugged him. That handsome boy was my only loyal friend. I could tell him anything and he didn't judge me. Tommy and I went on to have adventures, er, I mean accidents together. So often, due to his pacing background, my beautiful boy would gallop off in a frenzy with me on his back, to a finish line of his choice, not stopping until he was totally spent and covered in a white foamy lather. Many times, I'd fall off or would fly over his head as he'd come to an abrupt halt.

"Tommy, stop trying to kill me!" I'd say as I'd lead him back home, limping, my face grazed and bloodied, my arms, back and legs in severe pain.

In that same bush land, Gaby and I would gather mushrooms, swim in the creek, catch tadpoles, and paddle our home-made pontoon, "The Gabgaikar," in the shire water catchment area nearby. We looked forward to the summer rains which brought flood waters flowing down our street, as it searched for lower levels to be dispersed onto farmland nearby.

It had always been quite the spectacle! So often the little green cottage at number 10, the lowest point of the street down the road from us, would get flooded out. We'd watch on as the family fought to save their possessions. We'd see the aftermath of devastation as the flood waters subsided. We'd feel sorry for them as they'd hang their possessions over the fence to dry, hose out their house and spend weeks cleaning up the foul-smelling debris that had entered their house and yard uninvited. Yes, it had been quite the spectacle, almost an annual tourist attraction!

Thank God we didn't live there!

Chapter 7

To Sir With Love

I couldn't cry. I couldn't believe he was dead. In my mind's eye I saw his handsome forty-something-year-old face, his well-chiselled jawline, his charismatic smile showing the glint of gold of his front tooth implant and his bright shining eyes. Everywhere I gazed, I saw him: on the ground as I walked slowly behind the funeral cortege, in the trees as I glanced up occasionally to check how far I still needed to walk in my stilettos, and in the sky as I peered towards the heavens with the expectation of seeing his face peeking out from behind a cloud. For some unknown reason, this man was not dead to me.

***

"Karin, pull your socks up," said Mr Russell, my grade seven teacher, with a wry smile. I bent down to pull up my bobby socks, stretching them as far up over my ankles as I possibly could. He must have thought my socks were the fashionable Bermuda socks and they had fallen to my shoes. However, my socks were well-worn, loose-fitting hand-me-downs which kept slipping down into my shoes when I walked. How I had wished my clothing was more fashionable. How I wished I was pretty like my friend Kerry, well mothered like my friend Nola, or indulged like my classmate Elizabeth. Didn't Mr Russell realise that these second-hand socks didn't go up any higher?

That afternoon, like every day, on my way home after school, I called into the commercial laundry, owned by my parents, to announce my arrival. They had always waited expectantly for us girls to arrive, as on the far side of the large shed-like building, our chores awaited us. There were always piles and piles of washed and dried towels, sheets, pyjamas, underwear, and socks from the high school hostel for us to fold before we were released to go over the road to our home to prepare the evening meal.

It appeared my parents' laundry business was also the first port of call after school for many of the male teachers in Merredin. I would often feel embarrassed if they spotted me working in the back corner, so I would keep my head down and try not to make eye contact when they came to collect their clean laundry. Fortunately, my father or mother would usually serve the customers, so I was left to skulk behind the huge piles of clean washing. However, this day, Mum was busy on the phone and Dad was out doing deliveries, when a customer came to the front counter.

"Karin," yelled Mum, which was my cue to drop what I was doing immediately and go to the front desk to serve someone. I glanced up and there was Mr Russell, my teacher. I just wanted to die. Darn, how dare he come to the laundry and catch me working! I felt that when I was completing my daily afternoon chores at the laundry, I was living my private persona. Just minutes before he would have caught me folding his own underpants. This was not cool! Without saying a word, I went over to the parcel rack, found his clean laundry all wrapped in a brown paper parcel, hurriedly grabbed his money, threw it at Mum, and raced back to where I was busy folding hundreds of boys' snow-white y-front underpants. I was always proud of how straight my stacks of folded laundry were. My sister Gaby and I would often make our work fun and have competitions on which one of us could make the neatest or the highest piles.

That evening, Dad mentioned he had had a lengthy conversation with Mr Russell about me that morning when he'd dropped off his dirty washing.

"I told him to tell you to pull your socks up if you didn't perform to your best," he said.

Well at least that explained that comment he had made about my attire. After that day, it appeared Mr Russell began to take an active interest in my academic ability. I soon felt valued, nurtured, and even favoured. Secretly I believed I was singled out for privileges and respect. I had never felt so special in my entire life. With that type of treatment, I thrived. School was a wonderful place to go every day. I didn't mind working hard at the laundry, as I knew the next day, I would be going to school to see the wonderful Mr Russell.

My Dad, a chess enthusiast, would ask many of the teachers, Mr Russell included, to come to our home for a game of chess. Mum would cook one of her tasty German meals. We girls, so well behaved, would clean up after the meal without being asked, and the men would retire into the lounge room to smoke and play chess. However, this was my secret, my private life. I didn't tell any of the kids at school, for fear of being accused of being teacher's pet. These teachers became good friends of my father and even helped him dig a swimming pool in our back yard. Many a barbeque and brown bottles of beer were enjoyed during these times.

Thanks to Mr Russell, grade seven was the best year of my entire school life. I felt he brought out the best in me academically and psychologically. My self-confidence grew as he would challenge me to take the grade one class when their teacher was absent. He'd ask me to take the class spelling lesson when he needed a smoke (yes, 1966, teachers got away with these types of antics) and he would ask my opinion on many matters concerning the class and my fellow students. I thrived. This was the way I liked to be treated and I loved him for it.

Doubt still haunts me to this day as I was announced 1966 Female Dux of the School. Was it because I was academically number one, or was it because I was the unofficial teacher's pet? Either way, my name is still on that Honour Board.

Thanks to my parents' friendship with Mr Russell, he never left my life, even though he moved on to a metropolitan school the following year. Three years later, on the day the Junior results were published in the newspaper, he sent me a telegram praising my efforts and said he would see me the following day. True to his word, Mr Russell and his lovely lady friend, Trish, arrived the following day and stayed the night at our house.

What a joy to have my favourite person in the entire world back with us again. Trish was also the most beautiful lady one could meet. I loved him, and I loved her immediately. Once again, I kept quiet about my surprise visit as I didn't want my school friends to comment. I didn't need their opinions, positive or negative!

When I married, my husband Ray and Mr Russell hit it off and by then I had formed a friendship with his wife Trish. As life panned out, they had two daughters around the same ages as my children Glen and Erica. We visited him and his family in Perth on many occasions and our children would swim together in their huge pool.

***

"Karin, Karin," yelled my mother as she beat on my backdoor. Mum stood there ashen faced.

"Mr Russell has died," she said.

I couldn't believe it. I didn't want to believe it. Not that beautiful, beautiful man with those gorgeous little girls and that sensational wife. I knew he had been ill with leukemia, but I hadn't realised his death was imminent. That man had been my inspiration, my shelter from the storms of my girlhood, my idol, my hero.

The legacy of Bill Russell lives on through his wife Trish, his daughters Melissa and Kylie and his eight grandchildren, several of whom have an uncanny resemblance to him. To this day, I have an indelible picture of Mr Russell in my mind and am forever thankful to him for being a key influence in my life. Always loved, never forgotten!

***

I placed a rose on his coffin before they lowered it into the ground. "To Sir with Love," I whispered.

***

That was my life as a child. Mostly work with intermittent play. Mr Russell was the one bright light of my entire 11 years of formal education. With working at the laundry part-time for at least six days a week, and being heavily disciplined, that one teacher knew of my private life, and offered me emotional support and encouragement throughout that year. As he got to know our family, he could see they were good people, but were on a survival mission. As a child, I was always reminded I should never discuss my home life with anyone. Until now, I have kept my secrets. *How guilty am I feeling?*

In memory of Mr Bill Russell 1937-1979

Chapter 8

Cinderella Meets Prince Farming

I'd walked home that Friday evening from my job at the R&I Bank, carrying a shopping bag with my latest clothing purchase within. Exhausted, I sat down at the table to join the family for dinner.

"Would you like to come to the Oasis Hotel with us tonight?" asked my married sister, Anne.

"I'd love to," I replied. I knew exactly what I'd be wearing as I had just bought the perfect outfit and was ready to try it out.

Bored, 17-years-old, and single, having recently called it a day with my eighteen-month on-again, off-again friendship with Peter, I was keen to get out of the house. I knew I wasn't old enough to drink alcohol, but that didn't bother me as I didn't even like the taste of it.

Preened to the hilt with my mop of shoulder length, curly brown hair, teased into a wild bouffant and my trim body tightly squeezed into my new one-piece wine red hot pants suit. Black knee-high boots hugged my slim legs, accentuating the shortness of my outfit. I'd smothered my lips in the latest shade of burgundy lipstick and highlighted my eyes with a deep blue eye shadow. I was ready for my first night out ever as a grown up.

I felt very self-conscious as the Oasis began to fill up with the who's who of Merredin's eligible girls and lads.

As I was settling into my first Coca Cola, the hotel's front door flung open and in walked a remarkably familiar, handsome young man. He glanced over to our table and nodded at my sister Anne, and then at me. I recognised him as Ray, from the farm up the road. *Wow, he's all grown up and not half bad.* His sister and mine had been friends for years, and both girls had spent many an afternoon hanging out at the Jarvis farm.

Anne had often spoken of the Jarvis boys. There were three of them, all good handsome, and all in the eligible age-group. Anne, at 19, had married the local Post Office Clerk. At that time, her husband was serving in Vietnam as a conscripted SAS soldier and was home on leave that week. My mother had secretly hoped one of her daughters would snag one of those fine Jarvis boys.

"You'd be set for life. Such a good, hardworking family," she'd often say.

Ray headed over to his friends who had congregated at the front bar, bought himself a beer, and turned around to look over at our table. If I wasn't mistaken, every time I looked up, he was staring at me. My heart fluttered. What's a girl supposed to do? *I know, play hard to get.* In 1971 all the groovy chicks played hard to get in the magazines I had read, and that night, in my hot pants, I was a groovy chick! I began to play with my curly hair in a coquettish manner, sneakily glancing over at him then quickly averting his gaze.

A young man from a neighbouring town interrupted my game when he came over and asked me to dance. *Blast, if I must, but only because he was kind enough to ask me.* I joined him on the dance floor and proceeded to work through my repertoire of go-go dance moves, ranging from Running Bear through to Hitch Hiker. I gazed towards the bar where Ray was standing, glaring at me. My dance moves accelerated as my confidence soared!

The young man with whom I was dancing asked if I would like to accompany him to a football social at the Towns Recreational Centre after the pubs" closing time. It was 1971, all hotels closed at 10pm. As a well-mannered, people pleasing, innocent country lass on her first night out, I said "Okay, but you are going to have to get my parent's permission first."

Unperturbed by this, and with Anne's approval, he drove me to my home, walked me inside to meet my parents who, at this time of night, were huddled up on the lounge watching TV, in front of the heater, in their pyjamas. *Great first impression!* Mum consented and told him to have me home by midnight.

On arriving at the Recreation Hall, my date knew nobody, and didn't know where to sit. The only person I recognised was Ray, who had also decided to attend the social. There were two spare seats next to his, so I asked if we could sit there. From the moment I sat down, Ray and I began talking exclusively to each other. We chatted about the farm, their trotting horses, my horse, his siblings, my sisters, his parents, my parents, his football, and my job at the R&I Bank. We chatted as though we had been friends for years. We were neighbours, had attended the same schools, he had been in many of my sister Gaby's classes, and we knew each other's basic family history.

My original date at some point gave up on me and headed off to find a more willing dance partner. When Ray noticed him smooching a local lass on the dance floor, he suggested that he drive me home. I thanked him for his consideration. On our arrival at my house, I invited him in for a coffee. In those days, coffee meant coffee. He accepted. We continued to talk and talk. My mother, who was semi listening from her bedroom just down the passage, wondered what I had found so attractive about the young man who had taken me out earlier that evening. She hadn't taken to him at all.

At sunrise, my sister Anne woke me, yelling:

"Who drove you home last night? Surely it wasn't that creep who escorted you. Who were you talking to until the wee small hours?"

There was joy, singing and dancing in the household when I told them Ray Jarvis had driven me home, as my date had gone off with someone else. Anne immediately phoned her friend Faye, Ray's sister.

"Faye, you'll never guess what? Your brother Ray drove my little sister home from a dance last night, and they ended up talking half the night. Mum heard them. She said they were both talking non-stop. He's even asked her to go to watch him play football on Sunday."

"Oh, my god, we'll be related. How fantastic is that?" yelped Faye, as both ladies celebrated their impending sisterhood via marriage. My mother was ecstatic!

"I've always wanted one of those lovely Jarvis boys in the family. You'll have a wonderful life as a farmer's wife," she practically cried with joy.

Pressure! However, not being one to disappoint my parents, I went along with the mission of fulfilling their dreams. My one and only night of freedom, at the age of 17, and my life's journey had already been mapped out by others. It appeared I was on the verge of making many people live happily ever after.

Chapter 9

The Wedding

"You've SINNED!" bellowed the pastor, in his usual boisterous, fear mongering, melodramatic manner.

"But…but we love each other," I whimpered, in my frightened little-girl voice. *Was I trying to convince him or myself?*

"That's not LOVE... that's LUST!" he spat, his arms stretched in the air, his head facing the heavens as though he were commanding a dose of hellfire and brimstone to be miraculously delivered upon me. As his anger subsided, he removed his glasses, rubbed his eyes, blew his nose loudly into his handkerchief, and bowed his head in bitter disappointment to consider the situation. He had obviously just received the most earth-shattering news of his life. Karin had sinned!

It had been my set task that evening to inform the family pastor that the wedding, originally planned for January 1973, had been brought forward and would now be taking place in six weeks" time, due to "a technicality." In our defence, we *were* left home alone, unsupervised while my parents had driven to Perth Airport to pick up my paternal grandparents who were making their first trip to Australia. My betrothed and I sat clinging to each other in stunned silence. Never in our wildest dreams had we ever imagined that the first time we had a crack at "you know what," I would become pregnant. We had survived the first year of shared celibacy, sorely tempted, I might add, but survived we had.

***

Just eight weeks prior to this moment of confession had come the marriage proposal. I was then 18 years old. My childhood dream was to become a nurse and, just hours earlier, I received a letter of acceptance into the nursing course and was eagerly awaiting the delivery of the parcel that would contain my new uniform.

Unbeknown to me, my practical, old-fashioned country boyfriend believed it was his duty to provide his future wife with a home. He had secretly purchased a modest house from his meagre, hard-earned savings, and planned to tell me when, and if, I accepted his marriage proposal. The proposal came as I excitedly babbled on about my impending nursing career. His silence and lack of enthusiasm was evident as I chatted about my childhood dream which was finally becoming a reality. Then, without warning, obviously afraid of losing me, he fumbled and mumbled his way through what appeared to be a marriage proposal.

"What about you and me? Umm, I thought we'd have a future together. Umm, would you marry someone like me?"

Did I hear that right? Was that a marriage proposal? No passion, no romance, and no words of love?

I sat in absolute horror as I digested what that question would mean to me. I suddenly went cold. I shivered as I felt my dream being ripped from me. I froze to the vinyl seat of his Holden HR utility. I wasn't ready for that. *Why now?* Just a few moments earlier I had been planning my career. I couldn't open my mouth to reply. I felt sick. This man before me was a lovely, simple soul.

I didn't know what to say. Whatever I did say or do, I could never hurt his feelings. The silence was long and eerie. To break the moment, and as if to further sell himself, he announced that he had purchased a house. Not a flash one, he pointed out, but a house he could afford, nevertheless. When he announced which house he had bought, I shuddered. What was I supposed to say? I said nothing.

My shy young man obviously confused my silence as a resounding yes and proceeded to tell me about the house and was offering free reign for me to decorate it. He told me how he came to buy it, how much it had cost, how excited he was that he had a house for us, and how great it would be to be able to come home to me every night. He appeared so happy. He was on the threshold of a brand-new life with the girl of his dreams. At twenty-one years of age, he had his life mapped out perfectly.

My body trembled. I was frightened. I was still shaking as he walked me into my parents' house and announced our engagement. My mother and father were absolutely thrilled, as they had always hoped to snare that hard-working and most agreeable young country lad into our family. That night, there was excitement, toasting and merriment in the family home, as my parents and my fiancé rejoiced, as they celebrated the impending union. I said nothing. I still had not said, "Yes."

I really wanted to become a nurse. This quiet young man beside me was a delightful, considerate man. I couldn't say no, not when he had bought the house and all. I couldn't hurt his feelings. I knew he wasn't a confident person, so I couldn't break his heart.

Before I could digest the reality of the situation, it was decreed that by the following weekend I would have a ring on my finger. The wedding was to be in January and the reception was all but planned, just a few minor details to be discussed with Aunty Lisa, the restaurateur. Mum was working on the blueprint, already in place from my sister's wedding some two years earlier. Everyone was so happy. At that moment, I felt responsible for world peace.

***

"Well, you must be married immediately, roared the pastor, having thought long and hard about the next plan of action, "and you will not wear a white dress as you walk down the aisle of my church. It must be a cream dress as you are no longer a virgin, and you must also ensure the dress is not flamboyant, nor will it be revealing."

Guilt ridden; I sat in silence. What did I know about wedding dresses? What did I know about homemaking? What did I know about being a wife? What did I know about having a baby? I hadn't realised it was so easy to get pregnant, not with that act. Surely that's not what everyone is talking about behind closed doors. Surely that ever so simple, messy, and quick act is not what makes or breaks relationships, destroys empires, or even keeps people entertained for hours.

Still living under my parents' roof, subservient to their wishes, I hadn't yet enjoyed my teenage years. I hadn't had the opportunity to climb any mountains, to swim any rivers nor to follow any rainbows. The only dream I ever had was to become a nurse, a career etched into my psyche since my tonsillectomy at the age of five.

It was made clear that I had made my bed, and now I must lie in it. Humbled to the point of humiliation, I went along with everything suggested. Even to having my mother's friend's daughter as my bridesmaid, not my own much-loved school friend who, as my mother pointed out, was too chubby to look good in a bridesmaid's dress.

I went for the simple, non-flamboyant, non-revealing white dress. Yes, I know it should have been cream. My first streak of rebellion! I conceded to all the wedding planning and preparation in accordance with my sister's wedding. However, I did assert myself on one minor detail, and that was to select the Bombe-Alaska for the dessert, instead of the parfaits and sparklers as featured at my sister's wedding. They had accidentally fallen over on the trays as the waitresses were making a grand entrance, unfortunately burning one of them.

I also went along with the hour-long sermon at the church, standing the entire time, while the Pastor seized the opportunity to instruct me; to wait on my husband hand and foot when he came home from the fields, to not complain about anything because I was just a woman, and the man knew best, so I had to be obedient to his every whim. Then, at some point, I plighted my new husband my troth (*and if you know what that means, I welcome you to tell me.*) I promised to love, honour, and obey in good times and bad until death do us part. Then as if to seal my fate until the end of time, the pastor bellowed his final parting threat:

"What God has put together, let no man put asunder!" I was then pronounced a married woman. At that moment, I felt the prison gates lock down all around me. My girlhood gone, my dreams shattered, my husband's property, and I was soon to become a mother. Tears of hopelessness welled in my eyes, which many mistook as tears of joy.

That scandalous act, forbidden to me just hours earlier, *yes, sex, I can say the word today,* was mandatory now that I was "signed up." The reception brought forth screeds of bawdy telegrams from well-meaning footy mates, all referring to the wedding night and how much fun it was going to be, and just how crippled we would be feeling the following morning.

My mother was ecstatic to see me wed. A married daughter was the hallmark of an accomplished mother. Her belief was; if a girl is not married by twenty-one, she would become an old maid, a spinster, and nobody would ever want her.

Pastor rejoiced as we left the reception to consummate the union. I was to become an honest woman. Yep, with that signed, officially witnessed special document in hand, I was now ordained by God himself to go forth and, was that to multiply or was that "to bonk?" I often suspected it was, to make more little people for his dwindling congregation to keep him in the fear mongering business. *Me facetious? No!*

***

However, if there was an upside to any of this, my German grandparents, who I had only met for the first time three months earlier, were present at the wedding. They had arrived on the day of our baby's conception and returned to Germany the day after the wedding. How's that for planning?

This is where I will leave this tale about an 18-year-old, reluctant bride, who never did become a nurse. Goodbye girlhood!

Chapter 10

Your Pain Is Real

As a young married woman, I moved from number 5 Colin Street down the road to number 10. Yes, you heard right; number 10. The house Ray had purchased without my knowledge. The house he could afford to buy with his meagre savings. It was going cheap. *Really?* I still had vivid memories of playing in the flood water just a decade before, and was fully aware my newly purchased, marital home was the lowest-lying property in town.

It was now the mid-seventies, and the shire council had publicised that the town's flood issues had been resolved. They had constructed a massive open cut canal along the rear of my bush playground of yesteryear. It was designed to carry the storm water through Merredin town, to drain into the newly built crow's nest dam at the end of our street.

*****

Sweltering summer days, high humidity, strong sultry winds, and black thunderclouds could only mean one thing. It was going to rain, or as the old-time farmers would say, "It's gunna bucket down!"

And it did. From 9am, on this day in February 1978, the heavens opened to spill forth its burgeoning reservoirs. The announcer from the local radio station, knowing the history Merredin had with flooding, invited the shire engineer to speak on the radio. He proudly assured us the town was protected from being flooded ever again due to the recent extensive public works program they had undertaken.

With the new town perimeter levy banks, and the clearing out and deepening of the open-cut canal, water would never be channelled into the town from out-lying properties again. All local water would flow freely through the town and out onto farming land to the west of Merredin.

"Don't worry, you'll safe," he assured the listening public.

Well, that's a relief! I'd seen rivers of ochre murky water flowing down that street for most of my life and as recently as the year before. I didn't ever want to experience that again. Fortunately for us, the previous year summer flood waters had just lapped at our front door, and only flowed indoors when sightseers in trucks drove along the road, creating a wake with their vehicles.

However, on this February, day by 8.00pm Colin Street was no longer visible, resembling a dark flowing river. Knee-deep water began lapping at our front threshold, threatening to wash inside, uninvited. My car had been taken to higher ground earlier in the day, and Ray had driven his utility to the farm and returned with a flat top truck. This was his back-up plan, should the water levels rise any further.

By midnight, the worst possible outcome eventuated. The water level had risen to the point of flowing into our house. The electric company had turned off the town's power. Bob and Maureen, neighbours from a nearby higher street, rallied with torches to assist. It was all hands-on deck! Battery lights flickered throughout the house as the men lifted our electrical goods and some furnishings onto the back of the truck.

"Take the kids out of the house," ordered Ray. The time had come for our two children to be taken to higher ground. I carried three-year-old Erica, while Maureen carried five-year-old Glen. What an adventure for them, to be woken up at midnight and told that they were going to Omi's, as our house was being flooded. They'd enjoyed it last year when the flood water had peaked at doorstep level at 10am. It had been so exciting for them as they splashed about and floated every one of their plastic toys all around our yard.

I laid the children down in Mum's spare room and headed towards the door to go back to face the worst-case scenario. My mother, by now a true Aussie country woman, offered to make a thermos of tea for the menfolk. I rested for a moment as she prepared her offering, while Maureen went home to check on her children. With plastic tote-bag filled with drinks and food for the boys in hand, I waded towards my house. The February night air was still warm. It was reported the barometer had read 99% humidity the previous day, hence the summer storms. I could see multiple streams of torchlight through the bare windows over at my place. All else was dark and eerie.

By now the water levels had risen to my chest height. As I reached the lowest dip in the road, the raging river of storm water lashed at my torso, threatening to drag me down into its murkiness and filth. I struggled to stay on my feet, refusing to give in to the force of the large volume of water. My physical and mental resolve was being savagely tested as I fought to remain upright. I felt a sudden blow to my ribs.

My god, what was that? By the faint sliver of moonlight, I saw a white, wooden guidepost redirecting itself from my path, to continue rushing along on its journey. The searing pain of that blow had winded me, and the weight of the gushing water was preventing my legs from taking the steps I so desperately needed. I willed myself, just one small step, recover, and then another tiny step. I glanced ahead at what I estimated to be fifty metres left to walk before I reached higher ground.

I knew every centimetre of this road. This was my street. It was not far to safety now, but I was fully aware I had to continue to fight for my life if I was ever going to make it through the relentless torrent. Floating debris carried along by the water continued to smash against my body as I slowly crept, breathless, frightened, and physically exhausted, towards my home. The street of my childhood that had once shown me the wonders of life, all those years before, was now threatening to show me the wonders of the afterlife.

By torchlight, I could see knee high water gurgling throughout the house, as it searched for an escape route. *Thank you, God, for getting me safely home, I silently whispered.* I was unable to tell Ray of my near-death experience as he had his own set of worries, so I just handed him his well-earned thermos of tea and the sealed container of cake.

With the rescue mission of our white goods, lounge suite and kids' beds accomplished, Bob left. Ray and I then waded through the house and sat on our double bed, where we just watched, mesmerised by the swirling water lapping around us. By 2am, the water levels had begun to subside. We were exhausted as we walked, hand in hand, over to my parents' house, where we quietly lay on the lounge-room floor, trying not to wake the household. We attempted to sleep, but sleep did not come. We were both in shock and neither of us wanted to talk.

At first light we got up, still in the same soggy, mud-stained clothes we had worn the night before and walked over to our once pretty little home. I had always been a homemaker and had taken pride in its cleanliness and presentation. With the use of paint, matching accessories, and a little flair, I'd managed to make our humble little cottage into a comfortable, welcoming home.

Ray and I both felt empty and forlorn as we surveyed the aftermath of the previous night's carnage. Black mud squished through our toes as we walked from room to room, surveying the damage. To knee high level, all walls were stained with a distinct dirty water mark. Randomly strewn about were clumps of straw, deposits of animal manure, wooden posts, and miscellaneous floating debris, all of which was blanketed in a layer of foul-smelling mud and silt.

Among the filth, I noticed books from my bookshelf had been dislodged, and now blended with the array of debris and sodden junk. I kicked over a random book to check if I had read it. The novel, entitled *The Getting of Wisdom* by Henry Handel Richardson, lay saturated in a concoction of brown slop. I hadn't liked that book much anyway. *Who would sell their soul to the devil, just to fit in with a bunch of up themselves city misfits?*

Within hours, the angels from my softball team and the saints from Ray's cricket club arrived. I had no idea who'd asked them to come, but they appeared, ready for some serious physical work. Once the carpets and debris had been removed and taken to the tip, the ladies commenced scrubbing the walls and floors.

"What would you like me to do now?" asked a team mate on many occasions.

"I don't know, and I don't care." Ungrateful? No, just shocked! I felt numb and didn't have the energy to feel, focus or direct. I couldn't cry, I couldn't complain, I couldn't even blame. This was country living in its raw state. Fortunately, my sister-in-law assumed leadership and directed all helpers.

Days later, several of the mothers from Glen's preschool remarked how lucky we were that we didn't need to be rescued from the roof, like some people in the Queensland floods. I was grateful. I was lucky, but I was still in shock.

It was more than six weeks before I again recognised my house as my home. However, I was still walking around in a dazed state, and had never cried. As days turned into weeks and weeks into months, a tight pain in my chest was making it difficult for me to breath. My weight had dropped, and I had become a recluse. I eventually made an appointment to see a doctor.

I sat down at his surgery desk. But before he could ask why I was there, I became overwhelmed with a wave of heavy emotion, broke down and cried. My body wrenched uncontrollably as I sobbed and sobbed. The doctor sat patiently for a considerable time until I was able to speak. I spluttered out my story about the shock of the floods. I told him about being stuck in the water and fearing for my life. I said I'd been told I was lucky because I didn't need to be rescued from the roof.

Once he was certain my tears had abated, he sat back, gazed across his desk at me and said, "If someone has a broken leg, you can only assume their pain would be great. You don't know, as you can't feel it, but you still allow them to grieve their pain. However, if you have a broken toe, your pain is still real for you. Don't let anyone tell you that you should not grieve your own pain because there are greater degrees of pain in the world. It's your pain, grieve it, cry about it, and let yourself heal."

People would often quote the saying, "What doesn't kill you, makes you stronger!" I was left wondering, at the age of twenty-four years old, just how strong I needed to be to get through my life.

Chapter 11

Just A Girl Who Can't Say No

Being helped by others in my hour of need catapulted this independent soul well out of her comfort zone. It was usually me who was serving other people. Didn't I go to friends' homes and help them clean up? Didn't I make the costumes for other peoples' kids for the fancy-dress ball? Didn't I take my iron and ironing board to assist friends with their stack of ironing? Didn't I make the profiteroles for everyone's functions?

For the first time in my life, I was at the mercy of other people's kindness and hard work. Seeing that band of merry workers shovelling sodden debris out of my house after the flood, gave me the strongest feeling of gratefulness. However, I also felt humbled and useless. Once I'd recovered emotionally from my shock, I set myself a plan of payback.

"We need someone to fund raise for the Crippled Children's Society. We need someone to fund raise and increase awareness for the Arthritis Foundation. We need someone to be treasurer of the steering committee to build a pre-school. We need someone for this, and we need someone for that," stated anyone and everyone.

My self-worth didn't lie in me being kind, intelligent, fun, honest, or just a great friend. My self-worth became all about what I could give back to others. As first-generation new Australians, it had been drummed into us that we should earn our place in this great country. We had to prove to others we were worthy of living here.

My own father worked over and beyond for his beloved Lions Club International. He spent most of his spare time giving back to his new country. My mother worked tirelessly for the Lutheran Church where she cleaned, cooked, fund-raised, gave of her own money to pay accounts, and always showed hospitality to the pastor and the congregation.

It was now my turn to earn my way. Here began my venture into organising, cooking, recruiting, selling raffle tickets, arranging dinner dances, holding auctions, and anything else I believed could raise money for one of my many causes.

One of my adventures was being an entrant in the Mrs Australia Quest 1979. A project where, as a twenty-five-year-old country girl, with no worldly experience, I always felt as though I was punching well above my weight:

Merredin Advertiser, November 1979
"There's More to A Quest Than Winning.

Karin Jarvis, Merredin's entrant in Mrs Australia WA Quest, writes: *On reading last week's Advertiser, I was quite surprised to read an article concerning the 10 state finalists in the above quest, and how Merredin residents were disappointed in the result. I am unsure whether this comment echoed the sentiments of all Merredin residents, or just those of the Advertiser's journalist, but I would like to tell you of all the many fulfilling experiences one can gain by entering such a quest.*

I entered this quest solely to raise money for the Crippled Children of WA. This was truly rewarding, as I was able to visit the disabled children at the Rocky Bay Village, and I found that we, the able bodied, could learn much about the true value of love and life from these bright, yet physically handicapped children.

Once fundraising, I was amazed at the genuine willingness of our Merredin residents who gave financial donations, baked cakes, donated premises for functions, sold raffle tickets, and generously gave me their whole-hearted support.

I was absolutely thrilled to be chosen as Mrs Mid-West, and to be able to qualify for the semi-final judging in Perth. I was even more surprised to have been selected from forty finalists as one of the final ten, to contest the title of Mrs Australia WA, in front of a television audience.

There was so much to gain just meeting these children and the generous people, as we all worked for the same cause. These wonderful experiences would make anyone a winner."

Glen and Erica, our two oldest children would often say they were brought up folding paper serviettes and wrapping chocolates in cellophane and ribbons for another of Mum's fundraisers. Ray was always a wonderful help as he would donate his time and energies in assisting me where possible.

In hindsight, I now see all the above was essential training for what was to come for my family and me.

Australia, the land of opportunity! Or so I was raised to believe, but everything was out of my control. Typical sun burnt country, we'd seen flooding rain and had also experienced droughts. It appeared that as soon as we got back on our feet from one weather or economic disaster, another challenge would confront us. This, if nothing else, brought me to my knees as I prayed for the rain to stop, for the rain to start, for the fires to be put out before they reached our farm, for the price of wool to go up, for the price of sheep to increase, and for the price of fuel to go down. I prayed and prayed, but to no avail. Life on the land became progressively harder.

When will my prayers be answered? I wondered.

Chapter 12

Time To Grow Up

"Has she had a sleep today?" asked the weary, hungry, and dirt-covered father. He'd been up since 5am to milk the cow before he headed off to work in the paddocks. It was ploughing and seeding time, so all hands-on deck were required on the farm until the job was completed. This meant early mornings and long days, stretching up to 8pm. That was on a good day if there hadn't been any machinery breakdowns.

"She's had a couple of catnaps during the day," I replied.

Alice was our third child. We weren't young amateurs. We weren't even young parents anymore. We knew about feeding, burping, and leaving a baby to cry itself to sleep. We knew this parenting stuff, but something was not right. As a mother, I was also aware all infants are different. My Glen was a great sleeper. You never had to tell him twice to go to bed.

A perfect child, one may say. Erica cried a lot for her first three months as I tried to persevere with breast feeding, as encouraged and coached by the local Nursing Mothers Group. Things finally settled down when the clinic sister reacted in fright at Erica's weight loss, and consequently loaded my car boot with boxes containing tins of Similac (powdered milk, high in iron, as advertised on the label).

"This will make her gain weight," she insisted. "Put her on this immediately and stop trying to breastfeed her," were her parting words. Erica never had a problem with sleep again as from that day on she wasn't being starved! Today, Erica jokingly says, "Well, that worked, I'm still a good eater and it certainly made me gain weight. Darn that clinic sister!"

Glen was eleven and Erica nine, when I felt a strong yearning to be pregnant again. Ray was not so keen as he knew the farm might not be able to support another mouth. However, in my salesperson fashion, I managed to convince him of my fervent desire. Reluctantly, he conceded.

Obviously, falling pregnant had never been an effort for me, and within four weeks I was quietly celebrating my pregnancy. However, no one celebrated with me. The folks on the farm said I was mad as there were already too many people reliant on the property. My own parents were angry as they had finally reached the time in their lives where they could travel and were planning to spend a year in Europe.

Ray and I felt like it was us against the world. So together, we made a pact; we would love our little child and would do the best we could to ensure he/she (I always believed it would be a girl) had happiness and love in her life. We didn't need anyone. We would work it out ourselves.

Consequently, when Alice wouldn't sleep, we couldn't turn to anyone. Ray would not mention her problematic behaviour to his family, as we knew they would have thought that it served us right for bringing her into the world. My own parents begrudged having another grandchild, as my mother had often told us that two children from each of her daughters would be enough. There I was, once again, the black sheep of the family, daring to bring another child into the world, giving her a seventh grandchild.

But what to do with a screaming baby? Ray and I eventually worked out that if we wrapped her up warmly, placed her in the pram, and walked around town for at least an hour, she would eventually go to sleep. We also worked out that if we walked along a corrugated road, she would get to sleep even quicker. Rain, frost, windstorms, dust storms and if we were lucky, a fine night, Ray and I could be seen walking around Merredin at 10pm trying to get our little princess to sleep.

Sometimes she would wake up at 2am and even though we would attend to her physical needs, she would scream for another hour before we would be forced to repeat the entire process. We couldn't leave her to scream much longer as the other children needed to sleep, and so did we. If we chose to allow her to cry, she screamed for a considerable period. She would work herself up into a frenzy, and hit her head on the cot, almost as a demonstration of defiance. By the time we conceded to picking her up, she was overheated, covered in mucus, had the look of hate in her eyes and had red welts on her tiny body.

In my 12 years of motherhood, I had not come across this before, nor had any of my friends. Their babies were sleeping through the night without any problems. I brought her behaviour to the attention of the clinic sister who told me to just let her cry. I couldn't get her to understand that Alice didn't cry, she screamed, and not just for 20 minutes like the average baby.

I made an appointment with her doctor who prescribed a sedative, popular at that time. Disaster struck! The medicine, which was supposed to put her to sleep, gave her days of being awake and not just being awake, this substance made her over-alert. It was like having a screaming baby on steroids. Ray and I felt alone. We couldn't go to the family, we couldn't depend on the doctor for advice, nor could we inflict our friends with our problems.

All this time, Ray and I were struggling with finances. It was true, the farm could not afford another mouth to feed. As for any plans for our children's higher education, well we didn't have any. We feared our house being flooded out again. We feared letting our much-loved children down. Three children; not one, not two but three (the third, with issues, it seemed). We feared failure! This could not be Ray's family's problem. This could not be my parent's problem. This was our problem, but I made it my problem.

The farming economy in 1984 was in decline. Drought had set in. Bank interest rates were at 24 per cent and were crippling even the most astute farm operator. Farmers were walking off their properties in droves. Front page stories of the local weekly newspaper showed images of destitute farming families, standing in the middle of their sparse wheat crop. A tale of farming woe would follow.

I made a note to self: *If my photo is ever to be published in that paper, it must be a good news story. An article depicting remarkable success. I will not allow myself to get so low! I will not blame the weather, the banks, the family, or anyone else. I will take responsibility and take positive steps well before my life gets to such an abysmal state.*

It was time for Ray and me to grow up!

Chapter 13

The Journey

Tears gushed as the fear of the unknown overcame me. *What will my future be? I'm so scared. Just keep your eyes on the road, look forward and don't look back,* I ordered myself. *Please God, keep my hands on the steering wheel. Please keep this car going forward. I must dream of the things I want for my family, if I don't, I know I'll turn back. Oh God, I'm not sure I can do this.* Tears cascaded down my already saturated face, dripping onto my clothing. My burdened heart heaved as I forced myself to recall why, yet again, I needed to be so strong.

*****

Just a matter of minutes before, my husband and our three children had lined up to wave me farewell as I prepared to drive the 265 kilometres to Perth to start a new life in real estate. Yep, real estate! That was going to provide me with an income to raise our family. I had been told, by selling real estate, one could achieve all one's financial goals. The world, apparently, could become one's oyster.

As I drove slowly from the town, I recapped the course of events that had brought me to this point in my life.

According to my migrant parents, I was living the great Australian dream: a husband, three kids, a house, and a dog, all before I was 30 years old. However, in my spirit, I felt only desperation. It was disheartening to dream, futile to plan, and hopeless to even imagine a life beyond the boundaries of Merredin, my hometown. My life so far had been one of just wishing for a better life and praying to the God of all things agricultural to have mercy, and grant us a decent harvest, so we could at least eat.

Then one day, exactly two weeks earlier when I was watching television, a program on goal setting grabbed my attention. It was a whole new concept to me, but nevertheless, I cooperated with the instructions given by the presenter.

"Write down what you believe you should be earning in a year" he said. *Easy! Given that I was several local organisations president,* *treasurer, chief cook and/or bottle washer, I wrote down $40,000.* I paused as I tried to image which business in town would pay me this exorbitant wage. *Well, a girl can dream, for this exercise anyway.*

"What sort of work would you like to do to earn this fee?" he continued. *My goodness, how would I know? But I'll play the game. That's easy: with my community activities, organisational skills, and my fundraising abilities, I should be doing a public relations type job. Gee, I'm on a roll here.*

"What type of accommodation would you like to live in?" was next. Not that there was anything wrong with my humble three-bedroom asbestos cottage, but I envisaged myself in a 4-bedroom brick and tile home.

"What education would you like for your children?" he asked. I wrote: the best school in the area which would give them opportunities to become the best people they can be. I had never thought much about my children's future, but it seemed right to dream on for their sake. To date, just feeding my kids had been foremost on my mind.

I certainly had never contemplated sending my children to private schools in the city, unlike one of Ray's brothers, whose two high school aged children were already at boarding school, with the two younger ones due to commence within a year or so. *Goodness, we could never afford that!* I was still cringing about the cost of the grey school shirts required for my son, who was due to start at the local high school the following year.

I enthusiastically answered all the questions as I fantasised about my ideal life, something which I had failed to think about before that day. I then followed the instructions: Give the same questions to your partner, and let them write their answers, with no prompting or criticism from you. Once completed, both questionnaires were to be placed in an envelope, forgotten about, and voila, our lives would change! *How easy is that! Nothing to lose here!*

That evening, I urged Ray to complete his list. I was astounded to learn, for the first time in our twelve-year marriage, his needs were so simple, and he was already living his dream. However, after a little thought, he decided he would like to double his income to $20,000 and would prefer to oversee his own business instead of being at the mercy of his older brothers' business decisions. But yes, sport, golf, time with the kids, potter in the garden, work hard, and maybe even have a holiday every now and then. I showed him my answers.

"Who the heck in town would pay you forty grand, and what's wrong with this house or the local high school?" he gasped. Undeterred by his lack of faith in the system, I carried out the final instruction by placing both answer sheets into safe keeping.

The following day, I found myself chatting to a stranger who asked me how the farming season was going. I mentioned that I really needed to get a job, so I could contribute to the family income. I explained I had no idea of what type of work I could do, as I could not envisage myself in any of the local retail positions, and I'd never learnt to type which would limit my employment prospects. Then, unexpectedly, the man said:

"I think you'd be successful at selling real estate."

I didn't comment, as I had no idea what he was saying. In my hometown, selling property was a job for the stock firms, not for an inexperienced young woman. As he walked me to my car, he patted the bonnet of my immaculate, shiny blue Ford Fairlane and said,

"Yep, I can just see you selling real estate in this." I mentioned that conversation to Ray, who surprisingly encouraged me to do some research.

The following Monday, we travelled to Perth to speak to James, the Principal of a real estate company, I'd randomly phoned, who surprisingly showed an extraordinary interest in me. At the conclusion of the two-hour interview, he announced: "I want you to work for us."

He obviously had detected an innate talent in me, yet to be unleashed. Before I had time to comprehend the magnitude of my actions, I was booked into the Real Estate Course in Fremantle TAFE, which was to commence the following week, and was being driven back to Merredin along with my hungry, screaming baby.

Oh, my God, what have I just done? I finally paused to ask myself. *I have a 13-month-old baby, still being breast fed, a 10-year-old daughter, a 12-year-old son, and a husband who depends on my support. To make matters worse, we have a house that's been flooded out several times. Who's going to want to buy that? What on earth was I thinking?*

I started to cry. In fact, I sobbed all the way back home to Merredin, as I contemplated my impossible dream. I was still crying when we collected Glen and Erica from my parents' house. I broke down and told them what I had done. That night I continued to cry and question my sanity. *What am I doing? How bad is my timing? How bloody stupid am I?*

The following morning my parents arrived at our doorstep. As they walked into our house, my dad spoke first.

"Okay, now sit down, shut up and just listen," he ordered. "We're going to give you an opportunity to make something of yourself. Ray and Mum will be look after the kids. Wean that baby! We'll put our caravan in your sisters back yard in Thornlie for you to live in. You will go. You will be successful, and you will not fail. Ray can sell the house and after harvest he can leave the farm and bring the kids to join you."

In those days, my German father's orders were totally non-negotiable. My father and mother had not left their homeland for Australia just to become battlers, and they would not give me permission to become one either.

I spent the following few days saying goodbye to my friends and in-laws, who were positive I'd be back within the month as real estate was apparently full of sharks, many had said. Everyone had a story about someone they knew who had tried real estate and failed.

"Absolutely no-one buys houses from women," said my father-in-law. Other well-meaning friends pointed out what a terrible wife and mother I was. However, I knew one person in real estate and, from where I was sitting last Monday morning, he appeared to be extremely successful. Perhaps my ignorance was bliss, or was I just a desperate, gullible woman with an impossible dream?

Exactly one week later, sobbing my heart out, I drove towards the unknown which awaited me in Perth. My journey had just begun.

Chapter 14

The Dream Job

"Okay, there's sixty of you here and in six months, there'll be two of you left in real estate," announced the first lecturer at the real estate course. I glanced around the auditorium, glaring at faces as I wondered who the other survivor would be.

"And" he continued, "if you think you will be able to get away with any shonky dishonest dealings in this industry, then let me tell you, there is a special wing at Fremantle Prison which houses real estate agents only.

I had not ever questioned, until this moment, why the survival rate was so low, nor did I know there could be "shonky dealings" involved in the industry. *Goodness, this is serious stuff. I'd better listen and learn.*

Thus began my learning curve about Torrens Titles, Offer and Acceptances, Contract Law, and other legalities in relation to the industry. I must admit I found the course to be difficult. It was like learning a whole new language. I wondered if I'd even pass the exams. What made it worse, my breasts were hurting as, just days before, I had walked away from breast feeding my baby. How embarrassing if I had a leakage! How embarrassing if I failed the exams!

My fears were abated when my name was called out on the Pass List. I couldn't believe it: so many had failed! I excitedly phoned James, my new employer.

"I passed the exam. I'm ready to start selling real estate," I blurted out over the phone.

"Well done. I knew you could do it. You'll be working at our South office. I'll let Geoff; the manager know. Be there by 8.30am on Monday morning," he instructed.

I was so eager; I could hardly contain myself. I made special preparation for my first day of work, not only with my grooming, but also with my real estate sales kit, which consisted of a new plastic file, a ruler, and two new black biros. On my first day in real estate, I walked into my new office, wearing my best black skirt, a green blouse, black stockings, and black high heeled shoes. The look of an excited child beamed from my face, as I entered that doorway clutching my plastic paraphernalia.

"I'm here," I announced. "What would you like me to do first?"

Geoff, the manager, a tall distinguished looking man in his early fifties, peered down his nose at me and said: "Grab a coffee and we'll have a talk."

"Coffee? Talk?" I exclaimed. "I'm not here to drink coffee. I'm here to sell real estate."

"Well, the first thing we need to do is to knock a bit of that exuberance out of you," he replied in a smug superior manner. The sales team sniggered as I was promptly put in my place.

Well, you can try to dampen my exuberance, but just watch me you self-righteous mob. I'm not here to sit around drinking coffee. I'm here to succeed in real estate. I must succeed in real estate. My entire family is expecting me to change their lives.

I soon learnt the harsh realities of the job. No-one was going to give me anything to get me started, so it was up to me to work out how to get a listing and then how to sell it. That's real estate! I discovered the best way for me to launch my career was to accost people as they scanned house photographs in the office window. I'd ask if they needed help and quite often, to my surprise, they would say *"yes"*. It was then up to me to ascertain their requirements, price range, and to plan an itinerary of homes for them to view with me. Easy? No!

On recognising my work ethic, a several of my colleagues asked me to open homes for them on the weekends. This was a wonderful opportunity for me to source buyers and to ask for appraisals, thus opening doors for me to build my own portfolio and subsequent sales.

I adapted to real estate like a duck to water and worked seven days a week to prove my competence to my employer, my family and most of all, to myself.

Within weeks, my mantra was, *I am not judged by the number of times I fail, but by the number of times I succeed, and the number of times I succeed is in direct proportion to the number of times I can fail but keep trying!*

I also learnt that one doesn't try real estate as real estate tries you first.

That initial enthusiasm did not wane as my competitiveness soared. In my first month, I managed to make four sales, which was a rare feat, winning respect, or was it envy, from my colleagues.

My success also attracted the interest of James, the Company's Principal.

Chapter 15

The Getting Of Wisdom

"Hello, Karin speaking," I sang in my newly perfected professional manner.

"I'd like to take you to Kwinana and Waikiki to introduce you to the southern office sales teams." The caller didn't announce himself, so I was expected to recognise the voice. It was James, the principal on the line.

Thinking it must be mandatory for all new metropolitan sales representatives to meet the company's entire team at some point in their careers, I decided to go, and told Ray, who was in Perth for a weekend visit. He agreed that I must do as the boss asked, to enhance my likelihood of success in the real estate industry.

What a terrific opportunity to wear my brand-new crimson mohair jumper, I thought, as I hurried to get ready to go and meet "he who must be obeyed."

My body felt enveloped by the deep comfortable luxurious black leather upholstered passenger seat of his shiny blue car. Like an excited child in a new playground, I glanced around the interior in wonderment, straining my neck to view all angles of this plush European made vehicle. The centre console sported a black leather encased armrest with a car phone attached. Yes, a car phone! I had never met anyone who owned a car phone. *How impressive!* The side electronically controlled windows were tinted with the darkest black sun shield film. Even the front window was darkened. *Goodness, no-one could ever see in. I wonder if the tinting is even legal in Australia.*

The conversation on the trip south was very subdued, as I stuttered and stumbled with small talk, trying to make myself sound knowledgeable. How privileged did I feel, sitting in that flash car, and being driven by a very handsome middle-aged man, whom I believed to be real estate royalty.

On arriving at the Kwinana office, James asked me to stay in the car, and went inside alone. *He must be going in to tell them about me*, I thought. Within minutes, he stormed out, ashen faced, with a look of carrying the worries of the world on his shoulders. Saying nothing, he drove to his Waikiki Office, some twelve kilometres further down the road. Again, he left me sitting in the car and went inside. Within minutes, he came back out with that same look of excruciating pain on his face. *Oh, my goodness, do I ask him if he's all right? What do I do?*

Once again, saying absolutely nothing, he started to drive his car further southward. I recognised the area as being on the road to Mandurah. *I didn't know he had an office in Mandurah.*

He didn't appear ready to talk. However, at some point, I just couldn't help myself, and broke the strained silence by uttering "Are you Okay?" He told me that several of the successful sales representatives from both offices had just resigned, and this was why they had wanted to see him in person. *Oh, what nasty people. How can they do that to this lovely kind man?*

With little or no further conversation, he continued to drive southward, well past Mandurah, and eventually ended up parking in the rear yard of a riverfront house in Yunderup, some fifteen kilometres further up the road. He told me to get out of the car, as he wanted to check something, in this, his holiday home.

As instructed, I got out and went inside with him. Once inside the house, without warning, he turned towards me and pushed me back against a solid kitchen table and started to grope at my body. As an unworldly country-town girl, this scenario was completely unfamiliar territory for me, and all I could think about were my milk engorged breasts and my nursing bra. I had only recently stopped feeding my thirteen-month-old baby, plus I was wearing my most unflattering cotton-tail knickers. Not a suitable time to be contemplating a fling, not that that was even on my radar. I promptly extricated myself from his grip, and ran outside, back to the car. He came out seconds later.

"Is that what you do with all your new reps?" I asked. I chose not to make a scene as I believed I was on the verge of an exciting new career. I had already sacrificed so much, and I didn't want to blow it by sounding immature.

"No, I was just overcome by the news about the sales team resigning," he said as tears welled in his eyes.

I suppose that's a fair enough excuse. What did I know?

Driving back to Perth, silence prevailed. *Was I supposed to have returned his passion? Was I really expected to have had sex on the table at the holiday shack? I really don't know much about hot lust, short of what I'd read in a few Mandingo books, my only source of the seedy side of sex education.*[2] *Besides, I've been married for 13 years, and had never had a man force himself on me. Gosh, all I want to do is sell real estate and make money to support my family. How childish do I feel?*

At one point he stopped the car by the side of the road near a sign advertising *flowers for sale*. He jumped out, ran over to the seller, made his purchase, and headed back to the car carrying two bunches of flowers. He handed me one of the bouquets. I leant my head forward to give the customary gratuitous sniff and was instantly taken aback by their strong putrid smell. With tears in my eyes, I began to cough and splutter as the rich earthy perfume overwhelmed my senses.

"Boronia! My wife loves Boronia," he said. *Well, guess what? I hate flowers and now I hate them even more. I particularly hate Boronia!*

I felt ungrateful as I clumsily stashed the bouquet down near my feet. A reaction which did not go unnoticed by my new boss.

On arriving back at head office, he told me to come upstairs to collect the inspirational reading material he had recently promised me. I tentatively followed him upstairs.

Within seconds, while walking past the photocopier, once again without warning, he shoved me against the machine and forced his huge body against mine. Like a possessed animal, he poked his tongue into my mouth as he shoved his hands under my new fluffy jumper and roughly groped at my swollen breasts.

"No! Noo!" I screamed. I tried to push him out of the way but due to his huge frame, I felt overpowered physically.

How am I going to get out of this? I frantically scanned the room for an escape route. Thinking quickly, I dropped to my knees and started to roll over and over on the carpet towards the stairwell, some three meters away.

"No! Noo! Nooo!" I kept yelling.

Slithering down the stairwell in a very unceremonious manner, I managed to look up, and saw a hazy figure of a large man, amid a cloud of crimson mohair which floated through the air like tiny deep pink

---

[2] Onstott, Kyle. "*Mandingo,*" Deninger's, USA. 1957

snowflakes. I kept rolling down the stairs as the crazed man fell to his hands and knees as he struggled to crawl after me. At the bottom of the stairs I sprang to my feet, quickly glanced up, and noted the carpet, the walls and James's clothing were all blanketed with fine tufts of deep pink fluff.

My heart shuddered as I breathlessly ran back to where I'd parked my car earlier in the day. Once inside, I locked the doors and, as if in a daze, drove back to the caravan where my husband and children were waiting for me. First stop from the car was the green rubbish bin where I deposited the foul-smelling Boronia. I said nothing of the incident to Ray. I needed to stay in real estate. I didn't want him to worry or to lose trust in me. I had to succeed for my family's sake.

This was just my first lesson in "the getting of wisdom."

Chapter 16

The Price Of Success

Dear James
Thank you so much for your interest in me but I'm sorry, I'm unable to be a party to anything that would jeopardise my chances of success. I have made a promise to my parents, to Ray, and to my children that I will succeed in real estate and have already sacrificed so much to be in Perth to pursue my dreams. I choose not to go back to Merredin a failure. I ask that you desist your unsolicited advances towards me. Thank you again for your interest in me, and I ask that we keep our relationship on a professional level. Kind regards, Karin.

Right, that should do it, I thought as I hand-delivered the envelope with the enclosed note to his desk, and quickly made my escape. Two days later, as I was sitting in my office, believing I had nipped any shenanigans in the bud, when my phone rang.

"I am going to Hong Kong tomorrow, so I want to see you before I go." It was the principal. Thinking he wanted to apologise for his behaviour, I agreed to meet with him. However, I was surprised that the designated meeting spot, at the rear of an out of the way local strip shopping centre, was an ideal place to meet. It appeared clandestine to me, but I drove there as instructed.

Within minutes, his shiny car with opaque window tinting, pulled up beside me. He wound down the passenger seat window and signalled for me to get in. I did as I was commanded. *This apology had better be good*! Without saying a word, he started to drive. He drove out of that suburb, through the next suburb, and the next, and kept driving until we were on a deserted country road, some twenty kilometres from my office. Still nothing was said. *He appears to know where he was going. Perhaps he's driven along these remote roads on many occasions. Maybe he wants me to help him do an appraisal on a country property.*

Our conversations were always kept to a bare minimum and consisted of discussions on my prospecting initiatives, my current sales, and my impending sales.

Eventually, he stopped and parked the car at the side of a deserted road, removed his seatbelt, and faced me. He began to adjust his trouser belt. Thinking he would start the conversation once he felt more comfortable, I crooked my head to peruse at the desolate farm scenery to my left.

When I turned my head back to face him, I was shocked to see that he had released his penis from his pants. It was standing angry, tall, and proud. I grimaced as I gazed over. *What on earth is he doing.* I tried to behave in an adult manner: not let out a childish scream or make a fuss, like this type of thing happens every day. *I must be grown up about this. My future depends on my immediate actions.* He finally spoke:

"Now, I want you to knock the top of this, and if you don't, I will cum in my trousers, and will make you take my soiled pants into the dry cleaners," he ordered.

The full cost of my real estate career was growing by the minute. *What do I do? Do I perform like a child or as an adult? Do I go back to Merredin a loser, and tell everyone that I, too, had tried real estate but had failed? My family's future and my pride were at stake here.*

After he felt relieved, he cleaned himself up with his handkerchief, said nothing, and we drove in silence, back to my car. I felt relief to know he was going away for a few weeks. Perhaps he would have a long hard think about his extraordinary behaviour.

As the days and weeks went by, his appetite for me increased. I tried so hard not to think of the incidents, and each time, pushed the memory of filth and violation to the back of my mind. I didn't have the luxury of self-pity. There was no-one I could talk to. My church-attending family had grand expectations of me, and as far as I was aware, knew nothing of the ways of the real world, not this world anyway.

***

Months later, in a moment of weakness while talking to my mother, I related a watered-down version about the price I was paying for my family to be successfully relocated to Perth.

"All men are like that, but don't you go spoiling your chances of success. Ray and the kids are depending on you. Your dad and I have also sacrificed a lot to give you the opportunity to go to Perth," was her one and only response. Yes, they did help Ray care for the kids, and

Alice was a challenge for my mother, who was not used to problematic children. Mum had also cooked Ray's allocation of food for the shearers at shearing time, as it appeared his family at the farm were not going to let him get away with not contributing, even though he was working all day, something that shocked me at the time, and disgusted my mother until her passing. I also had the use of their caravan for six months which had placed their own holidays on hold. Yes, it had been a sacrifice for my parents as well. Never again was the subject spoken of.

Nevertheless, I could not help thinking my mother knew more about life than she had ever divulged. *Pity, she hadn't told me more*! I could only assume she had tried to protect me from the dangers of predators by scaring me with stories about dirty old men during my childhood. Until then I had not even heard of manipulative, quietly spoken, successful middle-aged alpha-males.

I alluded to my workplace plight to Ray who, for some reason did not want to entertain the idea of me leaving that company. I was doing well and was becoming renowned for my real estate selling expertise.

"I see your signs everywhere. You must be doing so well," so many prospective clients would comment as they signed their property up for sale with me. Success attracted success, it seemed.

Years later, I was to learn that Ray had been dealing with his own life transitional difficulties at that time, none of which involved me. A story that was to utterly surprise me and also give me an almighty wake-up call.

Chapter 17

Besties

"Okay, you're coming with me." I looked up to see Linda, my only female colleague, holding onto a wad of printed material.

"Where are we going?" I asked.

"Door knocking," she replied, in a matter-of-fact manner. I detected a fiery glare of challenge in her eyes.

Door knocking was the bane of every real estate representative's life. Everyone hated it! I hated it too, but at that moment I was simply happy for a friendly invitation from this chatty colleague, so agreed to go.

There began a friendship with this vivacious, well-adjusted, energetic, naturally friendly lady, in her late twenties, who appeared happy in her own skin. I learnt she was also a mother but knew how to put her children and herself first. She didn't seem to have that insatiable desire for success at all costs, which drove me. She was calm! If she made a sale, that was fantastic as, on pay day, she would then go on a shopping spree to Bay View Terrace, Claremont, one of Perth's ritziest shopping strips. It was obvious that her and my family's financial situations differed. I relied on my sales proceeds to pay the mortgage, the babysitter, the school fees, and the endless array of family expenses.

James's interest in me had been suspiciously noted by the shrewd Linda, as apparently, he'd only just started dropping into our branch every day, which was some ten kilometres from head office. She'd deduced his new routine had only commenced since I had joined the sales team.

"What's going on there?" she queried in a tell-me-more manner. *My goodness, she's perceptive!* It was so good to find an ally. She was non-judgemental, understanding, and so broadminded, qualities I had not found in a girlfriend before. From there on, she took it upon herself to protect me, ply me with alcohol, and comfort me, especially when I was seconded to be taken out of the toy-box to be played with by James. Linda and I became firm friends.

One day my new friend returned to the office after an appointment and handed me a sheet of crumpled paper.

"Here, read this. My client is going through a tough time and found this to be helpful" I slowly read the barely legible faded, type written verse on it. I cried as every single word resonated within my inner being. *This verse is for me*! I quickly set about making a copy. It read:

Comes the Dawn

(Veronica A Shoffstall)

After a while you learn the subtle difference
between holding a hand and chaining a soul,
and you learn that love doesn't mean leaning
and that company doesn't mean security,
and you begin to learn that kisses aren't
contracts, and presents aren't promises,
and you begin to accept your defeats
with your head up and your eyes open,
with the grace of a Woman,
not the grief of a child,
and you learn to build all your roads
on today because tomorrow's ground
is too uncertain for plans, and futures have
a way of falling down in mid-flight.
After a while you learn that even sunshine
burns if you get too much.
So, you plant your own garden and decorate
your own soul, instead of waiting
for someone to bring you flowers.
And you learn that you really can endure
and you really are strong
and you really do have worth.
And you learn and learn…

With every good-bye, you learn.[3]

***

As time went by, Linda and I began to share our history.

---

[3] Shoffstall, Veronica A. *"Comes the Dawn,"* a poem first published in her college year book in 1971

We were there for each other to pick up the kids from school, open each other's homes for sale, and watched after each other's properties when either of us needed a holiday. We even minded each other's children overnight. Our lives became intertwined. Our husbands became friends, and our children saw each of us as part of the furniture.

We had sat together as her mother lay dying. I was present at the hour of her mother's passing, an experience I'll never forget. I had the greatest respect and admiration for Linda, a nurse in her previous profession, as she lovingly washed and laid her mother out in her guest bedroom. Together we comforted her father as he grieved the loss of his beloved wife.

My friend was confident, outgoing, and a free thinker. Qualities I envied. I was still trying to break free of my strict workaholic upbringing, together with the religious dogma I'd been force-fed for most of my life. She'd taken control of situations in her own unique way; such as presenting an offer to one of my vendors when I was unavailable to do so. Okay, she did go to the owner's house to conduct business on my behalf, wearing only her bathers. No wrap, no shoes, just a teeny-weeny bikini. Not the professional attire I would have chosen but I was thankful the house got sold in my absence. I was grateful to her for arranging an immediate appointment with her doctor when Glen, who we discovered was highly allergic to bees, received a sting, resulting in his head swelling up like a balloon.

"I know a doctor; he'll see Glen now. I'll call him personally." It worked. The doctor met us in the car park, and promptly administered Glen lifesaving adrenaline shots.

Linda had the solutions to all my problems. She had sat with me, reading her book, for hours at the hospital emergency department. My abdomen was swollen, and I had been in excruciating pain for days.

"Let's not waste time with the local doctors," she said, "I'm taking you straight to King Edward Memorial Hospital for Women." Her quick thinking led to me being admitted immediately for ovarian cyst surgery. A major operation with the removal of the cyst and the ovary was followed with a two-week recovery period in hospital. Then it was bed rest at home for a further four weeks.

She even found the home we eventually purchased in Bateman. By then, we had sold our Rossmoyne home, purchased an investment property in Kardinya (as per James's advice) and were renting a house within walking distance to Rossmoyne High School.

"I've got a new listing in Bateman, and I think you should buy it. It'll suit your family, she advised. Well, I could not argue with that. It was perfect for us: affordable for our means, good floor plan, had all the "I Wants," and was in the Rossmoyne High School Zone. My family went on to live in that house for 23 years.

Linda and I even went on to be involved in the same car accident.

I'd become totally dependent on her. I needed her in my life. She'd got to know my every weakness, and eventually introduced me the best dress shops in town, encouraging me to spoil myself, which in due course, I did. Frequently! I could tell her anything. We were "besties," or so I thought.

Chapter 18

Fired?

"I want to talk to you outside," commanded Peter, the new office manager.

"Sure," I chirped as I briskly followed behind him. It was a ridiculously hot summer's day, and I could feel the perspiration drip from my body as we stood on the pavement at the front of our office.

"Your behaviour last night at the Christmas Party at the principal's house was abhorrent. My wife even commented on your disgusting behaviour. You were an embarrassment to this office. And what's more, you've corrupted Linda. She used to be so quiet, and since you've been here, her sales figures have gone down," he spat.

What was I hearing? Me, corrupting Linda? I hadn't taken alcohol to the party; Linda had sneaked some into the principal's alcohol-free Christmas show and had kept me plied with laced punch. Due to the heat of that December night, I drank whatever she handed me. Yes, we both danced around the house, but isn't that what people do at office Christmas parties? I'd been reading about office Christmas parties for years, and that was, supposedly, where everyone let their hair down once a year, wasn't it?

"We don't need people like you in this office. I suggest you get your things and leave now," he ordered.

I couldn't leave! I had to succeed! I'd put up with so much rubbish to get this far, and now he's firing me over something that wasn't even my fault. I could not believe it. I had nowhere else to go. I couldn't go back to Merredin as a failure. Anxiety overcame me, my heart palpitated, and sweat poured from my face. I felt my knees crumple beneath me as I fell to the pavement. I fainted in the full view of shoppers passing by. I came-to as Peter tried to give me a hand to pull me up off the footpath.

He eyed around and I could sense his embarrassment as he discovered I was heavier than he had anticipated. People stopped and stared. At that point, he went back into the office, and asked Linda to take my handbag out to me. I grabbed my bag, said nothing, ran over to my car, and cried all the way to the house I had recently rented, as I prepared for Ray and the children to move to Perth. I lay on my bed and cried some more.

I yelled, screamed, and cursed. *Okay, so what am I going to do about it? Am I here to sell real estate or just to mess around? Peter can't fire me, he's not my employer. Am I really going to let my first Christmas party beat me? Am I a winner or a loser?* Went the conversation between me and my higher self. Suddenly, clarity reigned: If I really wanted to be a winner, then I must do what losers don't like doing.

I got off the bed, showered, changed my clothes, reapplied my make-up and hit the road. In the searing December sun, I began to door knock every house in South Street, Kardinya, a suburb just three kilometres from my office. Due to the heat, my presence on peoples' doorsteps had been well received by many kind homeowners, who, feeling sorry for me, offered cold drinks and words of encouragement. I had also been asked to carry out many property appraisals.

I'd only sneak back to the office to have my paperwork typed up by the secretary, and always left quickly to meet up with my newfound clients. Then I would walk the pavements again. I spoke to no-one from the office. I had to succeed on my own, and in my own way!

I did mention the incident to James when he phoned to ask why I wasn't at the office when he called over the next day.

"Well, I thought you were cute. It was good to see you enjoying yourself instead of being so serious all the time," he replied. "I'll talk to Peter." Consequently, the infamous Christmas party was never mentioned again. Eventually Peter and I went on to form a professional respect for one another.

However, I did realise that it was time for me to settle down and take my work seriously. I wasn't there to have fun. I was there to save my family from financial ruin. Management had seen me as the next rising star and only a foolish principal would let a potential top money maker go. Disgruntled sales representatives often left and joined an opposition company, taking their existing clients and probable business with them.

I soon discovered the harder I worked, the more successful I became! I also found that success is a very lonely place. Others, except those who were profiting from my hard work, weren't impressed at all.

Many of my male colleagues would criticise me, call me a piranha behind my back and even said to my face:

"Go back to the kitchen where you belong. Go home, this is no place for a woman. You've got kids, go home, watch after them. Go home and iron your husband's shirts."

Within two months, my hard work had paid off, and I was named *Salesperson of The Month* for the entire company. However, I had now laid my trump card on the table, and thereafter, each month brought greater expectations from management, and I would set higher goals for myself. I had already discovered that my success was equal to the amount of effort expended and, for me, that effort inflicted overwhelming stress on my mind and body.

I did stop at one point, and that was to write a letter to the Merredin Newspaper with an article entitled: *Local Girl in the Million Dollar Club*. I attached a photograph of myself. The article appeared on the front page of that publication for all to see. Achieving my goal, a good news story in that paper, with me as the subject, was a dream come true. *Okay, now I must get into the Two Million Dollar Club. More pressure!*

Chapter 19

No Fan-Fare

The furniture van carrying our 13 years of accumulated possessions rolled on out of Merredin. That van held nothing precious, only humble items, such as things to sit on, sleep on and eat off, all being transported to our rental home in Riverton. The precious cargo: the three children were all squeezed into the front of the Toyota utility. Ray was at the wheel. He knew he was going to have to make a return trip soon with a hire horse-float to collect Glen's pride and joy, his horse Goldie. For now, one thing at a time.

There was no fanfare, no family waving goodbye, wishing him well, no goodwill handshakes from his brothers or father. No parting gift, no good luck drinks, nothing! It was a lonely scene as Ray drove out of Merredin, the town where he was born some thirty-six years earlier and where he had worked tirelessly since he was old enough to carry wood, pick rocks, and feed livestock.

Six months after I had left town to work in real estate in Perth, our much-flooded-out home finally sold for a pittance. The harvest now completed, a job in Perth on offer, a position at a well reputed high school sourced for Glen for the following term, and a modest house to rent all lined up, Ray was now free to leave, or was that "to piss off"? He was leaving the farm, empty handed. Although his name was still on all farm documentation, Ray was refused any payout or bonus to see him in a better position to start again in Perth.

"You came to this farm with nothing, and you can leave with nothing," said his father. His brothers, his equal business partners, chose to ignore the fact he was leaving, and nothing was ever discussed. The elephant in the room was ignored.

"He won't go. He wouldn't have the guts. He wouldn't be able to survive in Perth. He won't have fresh meat, milk, or eggs," said his old-time farmer father.

Ray was never one to make a scene, blow his own trumpet, or discuss his feelings. It wasn't in his generous yet stalwart nature. He just carried his opinions and his pain within. As son number three in that dynasty, he hoped there'd be a place for him, but had secretly always been ready for a reality check. He knew full well, one day the farm would not be able to support four families and the eight children who all depended on its production.

He had always believed that one of them was eventually going to have to make the decision to leave, and instinctively knew it would be him. He was the only one of the three brothers who had not built a house on the farm property. He purposely chose not to do so, as he was acutely aware that a house on the farm did not add value to the land, and his own personal investment could never be realised.

As it ended up, there were three spacious homes built on the one farm. A situation which, in time, was to become intolerable and a nightmare for each brother to claw back their personal investment.

Ray had loved the farm. He thought nothing of working a fourteen-hour shift during the seeding and harvesting months. He willingly attended the farm seven days a week to fix machinery, feed livestock, assist his father with his trotting horses, milk the cow, and do whatever was necessary to ensure the smooth running of the property.

Our son Glen also loved the farm, and when not at school would willingly get up early to accompany Ray to work. Glen was true farming material. Like his father, hard work and long days never perturbed him. Coming home with a grime smeared face, filthy torn clothes and an exhausted body was par for the course. No big deal! Glen dreamed of working alongside his old man in the future and together, even then, they were a formidable team.

* * *

What the heck am I doing? thought Ray, as he fought back tears. *Merredin is all I know. Farming is all I know. My children, my wife, this vehicle that I bought for farm use from my own savings, Karin's car, and $20,000 in the bank are all I have in this world. Not a lot to show, after working my guts out seven days a week for the past thirty-something years. Ray Jarvis, it's time to grow up. It's time to take control of your life and stop blaming your father, your brothers, and/ or the weather, for the fact that, in the furniture van ahead and in this little yellow utility, is the paltry culmination of years and years of solid hard work.*

He shook with fright as fear of the unknown entered his body. He had a new life to look forward to. He was on his way to join me in Perth. He knew he could never look back, nor could he ever go back. There was nothing there for him now. His future was calling, no, screaming, for him to keep going forward.

Goodbye my beloved farm! Goodbye all I have ever known.

Chapter 20

Mother Of The Year ... Not!

"See you kids. Have a wonderful day! I'll be back after school for your party, Glen," I yelled, as I grabbed toddler Alice, and headed towards the front door. My diary page for 14th April 1986 read: take Alice to day-care, carry out set appointments, complete paperwork at the office, shop for party food, and be home by 3.30pm to throw a birthday bash for my son's 13th birthday. Well, that was the plan!

Just as I was about to run out the door, my home phone rang. "Good morning, Karin speaking," I answered, in my most professional sing song voice. Yes, in those days, you gave everyone your home phone number.

"Hello, this is Jason Walker, can you come over now? I want to list my house with you, and you'll need my wife's signature before she leaves for work at 8.50am."

"Thank you, Jason. I'll be there shortly." I glanced down at my watch. *Right, it's 8.30 now, that'll give me five minutes to take Alice to day care, six minutes to drive to Jason's house, and nine minutes to write up the contract for signing. Gees, I hope the traffic isn't heavy.* An almighty dose of panic rose from the pit of my stomach into my chest cavity. Real estate sales, for me, was one of those jobs that, when a client said *jump,* I'd reply, *how high?*

A job which was not conducive to winning "Mother of the Year," but this mother's mission was to provide a home for her three children, and to give them opportunities that were not available to them in the country. After fourteen years of marriage, my husband and I had made the difficult decision to walk off the family farm empty handed, and we had vowed to start again. Failure had not been an option!

With Alice safely in the back, I threw myself into the driver's seat and slapped the car into reverse. The car was moving slowly when I decided to check the rear-view mirror, where I caught sight of Glen's friend Brett, who was slowly and clumsily peddling down my drive on his ridiculously undersized BMX bike.

Darn, he'd better get out of my way, I'm in a hurry. I don't have time to wait for the kid to use his brains and get out of my way, I grunted under my breath. I continued to reverse the car. Suddenly my concentration was interrupted by the sound of Brett yelling out expletives as he made the timely decision to jump for his life into the garden bed.

"Erica, Erica, Mum's just run over Brett," I heard Glen scream out to his 11-year-old sister. He'd witnessed the incident and now had his head stuck out of his bedroom window. I reluctantly got out of the car to see if Brett had survived the ordeal. Yes, he's fine, just a few scratches.

"Why did you keep riding down the driveway when you could see me reversing?" I snapped. "Glen come and sort Brett out. Get some band-aids for his scratches," I bellowed, as I raced back to my car to continue with my day, which, so far, was not going to plan.

And what a day it was! With that additional morning appointment and the associated extra paperwork, the last thing on my mind was Glen's party. To make matters worse, as I was about to leave the office, my phone rang.

"Hello, Karin speaking," I sang. I recognised James's voice on the phone.

"I want you to accompany me to an appraisal at 20 Riverton Drive at 3.45 this afternoon." Let me tell you, no-one, particularly a woman with a desire for credibility and survival in the real estate industry, would ever dream of refusing an invitation from the principal to do an appraisal at any time, day, or night. In 1986, women would lose the professional respect from their male colleagues if they used their children as an excuse for lateness or their inability to attend an appointment. Very few of my colleagues, and none of my clients, even knew that I had a 22-month-old baby.

"Thank you for asking me. I'll see you there at 3.45," I replied.

Once again, that dreaded surge of panic hit my entire being. So, there I was at 3.15pm doing a mad dash around the local Supa Valu grocery store, throwing the mandatory party fare into my shopping basket.

My heart was beating fast, and my mind went fuzzy with frustration as I sped home, where I was welcomed with the raucous cheers from seven 13-year-old lads. *Goodness, they're happy to see me.* No such luck, these were hungry teenage boys and were cheering because I had arrived with the party food.

I jumped out of the car and called out to Erica to help me to carry in the grocery bags.

"Mum, I can't open the door. You've parked too close to the car-port column," Erica yelled. *Bugger. I don't need this*! I quickly opened the driver's door, turned on the ignition, put the car in drive, or so I thought. I leant into the car and placed my foot on the accelerator to move the car forward, but, oops, I had accidentally put the car into reverse instead.

Then suddenly the car shot backwards. A loud car-crash sound rang throughout the neighbourhood. The opened front door smashed into the wooden column, breaking it, and bringing down a section of the carport roof. Fortunately, Erica just managed to duck out of the way as the roof tiles came tumbling down onto the car. The boys cheered on in unison. They were loving the action!

"How cool was that?" they screamed. Brett, who was in the crowd, was probably wondering what I'd do next to endanger my family and friends. Remembering I had an important appointment, I scrambled out of the car, gathered the grocery bags, and raced inside.

"Erica, you're going to have to heat the party pies and the saveloys, love. I've got an appointment, I must go now," I instructed. What's new? she thought. The 11-year-old was becoming used to me putting my work before the family.

I ran back out to my car to survey the damage. The driver's door was crumpled and was hanging on by just a bolt. The tiles on the car were messy but did not render my vehicle unusable. Thank goodness, I could still get to my appointment. With the help of the party guests, I tried to close the smashed door, but due to the extensive damage, couldn't get it to stay shut. Once again, I felt that surge as anxiety rise through-out my body. I needed my car, and I needed it now. I had all of three minutes to get to my next appointment.

"Ockie straps!" yelled Brett. "Right fellas, get your ockie straps off your bikes and we'll put Mrs Jarvis in the car and tie the door on." Just this morning I had doubted Brett's intelligence, and now he was my ideas man. His ingenious plan had worked. There I was in a battered, once immaculate shiny Fairlane car, being waved off to my appoint-ment amid the boisterous cheers of seven over-excited Rossmoyne High School boys.

"Gees your mum's cool, Glen. This is what you call a birthday crash, not a birthday bash" I heard one kid yell out.

Feeling totally frazzled, I arrived at my appointment on time, where the principal was waiting. His look of surprise and bemusement greeted me as he inspected the damage on my car. Overwhelmed with embarrassment, I executed a non-too sexy exit from the car, which involved climbing, bum up, over the console, onto the passenger seat. There, I managed to recover my dignity, before alighting from the car, elegantly dressed for success, in my high heeled shoes and classically cut business suit.

***

As the years rolled by, missing in action from my children's birthday parties and other milestones occasions was to become a given. I had clients who believed their needs were greater than mine, and I had come to accept this as truth. If I didn't bow to their every demand at any time, I was afraid they would leave me and find a more accommodating agent. God knows there were enough of us to choose from. Erica soon became adept in arranging parties, making lunches, doing the washing, and arranging her own transport to Little Athletics and Volleyball. Glen's special skill was to take Alice to the babysitters on the back of his bike and to collect her after school.

His bike was highly visible in the school bike compound, as it was the only one in the line-up with a baby seat. With the infamous Occy Strap, Brett had tied a milk-crate to his bike which was solely used for transporting Alice's nappies and toys back and forth. Glen loved to cook and would ensure there was a meal planned for us each night. Erica could throw a mean salad together which became her signature dish.

"What do you call this, love?" her father once asked, as he examined the roughly chopped assortment of every vegetable imaginable.

"Pick Salad."

"Why do you call it pick salad," he asked with a quizzical look, as if to say: what the heck are we eating?

"Well, you pick about, and hopefully you'll find something you like in there." Fair enough! That recipe and expression has survived through time, and we still smile as we remember its origins.

Grocery shopping had become a neighbourhood spectacle, as my older children would place baby Alice in a Cyclops trolley and drag her down the hill to the Rossmoyne Supa Valu. They'd pile her up with groceries from my list, and treats from theirs, pay for it with the signed blank cheque I had left for them, and drag it all back up the hill to our house.

Neighbours would often say they'd seen my kids after their weekly shop, and reported they could hardly see the baby amongst the groceries. It was also conveyed that the three of them would be eating ice-creams as they struggled to pull the cargo home. I didn't have the luxury of feeling guilty about my lack of parenting skills. I was a woman on a mission to provide her family with a home and a future.

Chapter 21

Ray's Getting Of Wisdom

Driving towards the furniture hire company, situated in Belmont, Ray felt like a fish out of water. *My goodness! Look at all these streets! Gee, they go everywhere. I'd better learn some road names. I don't want to get lost. My gawd, look at all that traffic!*

Arthur, a cashed-up ex-farmer from Mukinbudin, a farming community north-east of Merredin, now business proprietor, had heard through a mutual friend that Ray needed a job in Perth. Ex-farmers know the breed of a farm boy, and to employ someone with a similar work ethic to himself was like an answer to prayer.

It was 1986, and Perth and Fremantle were gearing up for the America's Cup Yacht Race. The city was buzzing. Arthur, an astute businessman, had cornered the market in the hire-furniture business, and was on the verge of expanding his operations. He had grown to the point of employing a Transport Manager. Ray was a shoo-in for that job! Arthur and Ray bonded immediately. While Arthur admired Ray's enthusiasm for work, where he would complete each task with tenacity and still come up smiling, Ray admired Arthur's ability to dream, and to bring his vision into reality.

Ray set about making himself the best transport manager possible. He started his career by driving the truck laden with hire furniture to domestic and commercial sites all over Perth. *Well, that was one way to learn the names of the streets*!

His mind would often wander back to the farm, as he thought of his parents, his brothers, and the rainfall. *They must be seeding by now. They had 20 points last night. I wonder how Dad is going, he's been sick. Hope Mum is dealing with it. I hope someone is killing meat for their freezer. Mum should get rid of that cow. She can't keep doing that every morning.* Then he'd miss a street turn and was forced to bring his mind back to the present, and his job.

The furniture hire business was booming. They were now branching into exhibition hire, commercial hire, domestic hire, and display hire. Time to employ more staff. Ray was promoted to the transport manager and was required to stay at the massive warehouse, where he would deal with the logistics, oversee the ever-growing fleet of trucks, supervise the cleaners, and instruct the truck drivers. Ray had three phones strapped to him and quite often, all would ring at once. He would troubleshoot, direct staff, and plan the logistics, all at the same time. He'd learnt to multitask!

Our son Glen was employed by Arthur a few years later as a truck driver's assistant. At 16, he was too young to drive. Not the father and son team Glen had envisaged, but a formidable team, nevertheless. Ray called those times the glory days of furniture hire. While Arthur dreamed of becoming the biggest and the best, Ray and Glen worked hard, as they played their roles in the vast scheme of things. There were deadlines, customers to deal with, paperwork to keep track of furniture to control, and exhibitions to set up. During these times, Ray ensured there was always laughter, jokes, and drinks for the boys, but that was after the work was all done and dusted.

Have you ever got to the point in your life when you can no longer face the day? Ray was fast approaching that time of his life. He was finding it increasingly difficult to work up a zest for his job. Why? One may ask. By this time Arthur, the dreamer, his mentor, and dear friend, had sold his shares in the hire furniture business to three new business partners. Arthur had chosen to enjoy the fruits of his long life, and had purchased a huge caravan, a holiday home, and a massive utility. His dreams had become a reality.

Ray had his own decision to make.

In Memory of Arthur Prior 1934-2016

Chapter 22

Paid In Full

"What's wrong with you now?" asked James impatiently, as he observed me, sobbing in the office, yet again. In the three years he'd known me, in his mind I was always whining or stressing about something.

"I've just received a letter from the Westpac Bank, saying they will take the entire proceeds from the sale of our Rossmoyne house to off-set Ray's brothers' farm debt. If they do that, all our hard work over the last two years would have been for nothing. Ray's never been paid so much as a dollar from them since he left," I sputtered.

Six months after I had, according to the towns' folk, deserted my family to seek fame and fortune in the city, our modest little flood-prone house sold for $20,000. I had managed to add to that amount from my earnings, and by the following February, with a small home loan, we purchased the worst 4-bedroom brick and tile home in Rossmoyne. However, it was situated near the best high and primary schools in the area and was just a short drive to my office.

It was one of those houses that not one of my clients wanted to buy, with smelly thread-bare carpets, stained brick interior walls, and heavy dark pine wood trim. It certainly was not fancy, but it was affordable. In my eyes it had good bones and was an astute buy. Most importantly, it did pass the first rule of real estate: location, location, location, and was just a short walk to the Canning River. With a lot of hard work, paint, and imagination, we had managed to uncover a gem.

By the end of my first full financial year of work, I had reached my goal of earning $40,000, and had my four-bedroom brick and tile home in the highly sought-after Rossmoyne High School zone. My initial aims had been achieved, and I believed I was on a roll. Ray had also achieved his target. Things could only get better!

Then came letter number one from the Westpac Bank, threatening to sell us up and take our house proceeds. The letter stated that the farm was in financial trouble, something we knew nothing about, as we had never ever had access to the farm accounts books. I recall Ray asking his brother on two occasions if he could bring them home for me to peruse. With my previous banking experience, I still loved a good ledger. However, his requests were repeatedly declined.

Ray and I made the decision to quietly sell our house, and planned to put the proceeds into a special account until the farm's fiscal crisis was over. Fortunately for us, the house sold quickly for a tidy profit.

On the day of settlement, a second letter arrived stating that the bank would not release the sale proceeds to us. My boss, James, on hearing of our plight, took matters into his own hands, and asked to speak to Ray. It was apparent that this was a job for the alpha males to sort out. He instructed Ray to meet him at the Westpac Head Office that afternoon at 4.00pm.

James and his friend John, both dressed in black business suits, were waiting for Ray, who was still dressed in his working clothes, a white shirt, and blue trousers, as he arrived at the bank's headquarters. They went in and Ray, unsure why John was there, introduced the principal as his real estate agent, and John as his friend, to the hierarchy of the bank. The six men sat around the board room table.

One of the bank's executives began to list the farm debts, and confirmed they would not be releasing our house sale proceeds to us. Although Ray had been instructed by James to say nothing and to let him, the eloquent speaker, do the talking, Ray, in his typical down to earth, no-nonsense manner, felt he couldn't just sit there and let a room full of suited men dictate to him.

"I've got no idea why the farm is in so much debt. I'd always been told we were doing all right. That's why I was upset when they wouldn't give me any money when I left two years ago. I thought I'd be making it easier on my brothers, as there'd be five less people dependant on the property if I left. I've not received a single cent from that place even after my thirty-six years of working there.

That farm hasn't contributed one dollar towards the purchase of my Rossmoyne house," Ray angrily blurted. "I left that farm empty handed, and if you really want something from me, then go up to the farm and take what you want. Take my share if need be. I don't really care what you do, but don't you dare touch my house sale money!"

At that point, friend John began fiddling with what turned out to be a microphone on his belt. One of the bank employees noticed this, and asked "What's that?"

John reached into his suit top pocket, pulled out a business card, slapped it on the table and announced, "Sorry gentlemen, John Lee, Channel 7 News. I've arranged for a helicopter to be in Merredin tomorrow and will ensure your bank receives publicity for taking the house sale proceeds from this hard-working couple. Great human-interest story, don't you think?

This obviously put the proverbial wind up the bank executives, who quickly excused themselves from the room. On their return, one of the men said,

"Look, we don't want publicity over this, so we've decided to release the entire proceeds from the sale of the Rossmoyne house to your client."

***

Lucky? No! I'd paid for that house in more ways than one. First with money I earned working seven days a week for three years, and the other I paid for in kind. James's debt to me was now paid in full.

It was time to leave his company.

***

It took me ten years of time and emotional healing before I could relate the story of my first years in real estate without breaking down in tears. Today, I hold my head up high.

Chapter 23

To Throttle Or Not To Throttle

"Take 17. Everyone say cheese…again."

"No, I'm not saying that" screamed Alice, our defiant five-year-old daughter.

"Well, just smile," I suggested, patiently presenting a picture of family bliss in front of the photographer.

"No, I don't like smiling."

"Just sit still darling."

"No, I don't like sitting still."

"Sweetheart, this won't take long. It's Daddy's 40th birthday, and it will be lovely to have a family photo to hang on the wall to remember his special day."

"No, I don't want a picture of me on the wall."

"I'm sorry sweetie, but the rest of the family would like a photo of us on the wall," I ever so patiently explained.

"Take 18," ordered the photographer.

Oh my god, 18 takes and he hasn't got a half decent shot yet!

"Alice, put those shoes back on," I yelled. "I bought them especially for today. We all have lovely clothes and shoes on. See, Glen, Erica and Daddy have new shoes too."

"I hate wearing shoes and socks," she interjected as she reached down and ripped off her new footwear and threw each article randomly around the room.

Will I pick them up and put them back on her, or will I just get on with the photography session? This guy's charging by the hour, and I'm fully aware there won't be many, if any, good takes at this stage, thanks to Alice.

"It's okay, take the photos," I instructed the photographer. "I don't suppose it matters if she is bare footed."

"Take 19." Just as he clicked his shutter, the momentary peace was interrupted by screams.

"I wanna go to the toilet."

I grabbed her hand and dragged her off down the passage. A few moments later Alice reappeared, smiling, now sporting a dark water stain down the front of her pink taffeta dress.

"Little bitch!" yelled her 15-year-old sister Erica, her patience now exhausted.

"Gees Alice, stop buggerizing," added 17-year-old brother Glen.

"Come on Alice, I'll dry you off," I said, as I try to salvage the family photographic opportunity.

"I don't want to be dry. It's too hot in here."

"Alice, if you don't sit down, shut-up and behave, I'll punch your bloody lights out." I shrieked in my familiar fish-wife voice.

Oh goodness, the pressure of the timeline, the heat, and the spoilt little brat is getting to me! Had I just blown my cover of play-acting the fully functional, happy, successful family? Is the photographer thinking I'm a cow of mother? Will he be charging me by the hour? Will he pack up his gear and depart, leaving us sitting on the lounge in our new clothes? Did I get my afro bouffant this high for nothing? But to throttle, or not to throttle the bloody kid? This day and every other day, that had always been the question.

Such was a normal day in our household. There was never a thank you, a please, a hug or a smile from Alice. Something wasn't right! Every day was a battle of wills, egos, responsibilities, and obligations. Every day started with a skirmish. Firstly, to get her out of bed, prepare her for school, to convince her she must go to school, to shower, to eat decent food, and go to bed at night. Tasks not one of us were ever able to master in a quiet peaceful manner.

Mealtimes were a battle ground as Alice upended her food, threw tantrums, kicked everyone, and chose to escape the meal table. If she liked what I had cooked, she'd grab her helping and disappear. If she didn't like the offering, she would have an outburst of temper before locking herself in her room. It was never a surprise to find food jammed in a pot plant, in her toy box, or thrown out of the window.

At this point, I don't really want to mention homework, as that word was enough to make the entire family's blood boil. It still does! Every reading book brought out the worst in Alice's behaviour, usually triggering an explosive cocktail of her own obstinance, and rage in her family. At the age of seven she was diagnosed with Dyslexia.

Glen and Erica lived patiently at the edge of these family dramas. Both siblings had a close relationship with each other and shared a common sense of humour. They were both self-confident, self-reliant, respectful in family and social groups, but had a low tolerance of Alice's antics.

To see the relief on their faces when their younger sibling escaped the meal table, accidentally fell asleep in the car, locked herself in her room, or watched TV on her own, was almost a joy to see. Both were then free to express themselves and lead the family in mealtime fun and laughter. Neither teenager could understand Alice's behavioural issues, and Ray and I didn't expect them to. Quite frankly, we didn't understand or tolerate it too well ourselves!

But what do you do? Every day began as a new day where we needed to put the pressures and disappointments of the previous day behind and start the day with optimism. Sadly, the new days didn't bring answers, respite, or reprieve.

Chapter 24

Change Is Inevitable

"Today, we're all going to view a house in Wilson," announced Nick, my new boss and owner of the company.

"Aw, I don't want to go to Wilson. I hate bloody Wilson," responded one bright spark of the team.

"We'd better go, to pay respect to the owner for giving us the listing," replied Nick.

This was a fun office. If we had something to say, we'd say it. If we didn't like something, we'd said so. If something was funny, we'd laugh out loud. I'd joined a jovial bunch. We worked hard, played hard, and still managed to achieve our individual set sales targets.

Life was becoming all I'd imagined it could be. I had finally found the courage to escape my old company run by the infamous James and had joined Linda just across the car park at a new real estate agency. I had two wonderful colleagues: Mike, an accountant who had sought a change in career, and my best friend, Linda. Together we were like the three musketeers. We assisted one another, covered for each other, and encouraged one another. Perfect!

"Okay, Wilson, here we come. I'll take my car," said Nick. The team and I climbed into the boss's luxury car. I sat in the front passenger seat, while Linda was in the back seat in between two of the other reps. There was laughing and joking as we drove along. *Oh, what fun we have when we check out new properties together*, I thought, as we zoomed through the suburbs towards our destination.

My attention was not on the road as I was busy, as per usual, checking for opposition real estate for-sale signs. If ever I saw an opposition real estate company's sign on a property I had appraised, I would feel totally sick, and ponder if it was due to my pricing, or had I just failed to impress the client with my professionalism, or perhaps, even, my femme-fatale charm.

Suddenly, the ear-piercing sound of metal smashing resounded through the air and interrupted my game of sign spotting. I heard Nick curse as his car began to spin around. As though in slow motion, I saw houses, trees, and the road float around me. I felt my neck jerk with that motion. Once the car had come to a standstill, the five of us sat motionless, in shock, as we tried to fathom what had just happened. We soon learnt that a load of Chinese tourists in a hired Nimbus had failed to give way at a stop sign and crashed into Nick's car. We all crawled out of the vehicle as Nick phoned the police from his newly purchased modern convenience mobile phone.

"Are you guys alright?" he squeaked, obviously in shock. By now, a female sales representative from the back seat was crying hysterically. The male sales rep from the rear was groaning, as he ran his hands over his shoulders, ribs, and head. Linda and I were in total silence and disbelief as we sat down on the road verge.

Well, of all the places to have a car accident, we were directly in front of a doctors' surgery. The doctors and staff came running over and escorted us into their rooms. Linda and I found this to be quite amusing and made wisecracks about the doctors drumming up business at that intersection. Linda and I were ushered into a separate room, with just one patient bed. When she felt dizzy, she'd quickly climb up onto the bed to rest. Then, I suddenly felt dizzy, so she clambered off the bed, and let me have a lie down.

Then she felt dizzy again, so I'd crawl off the bed. This bed rotation went on for a sizeable number of times. Hilarious, if it was happening to someone else! Once we were checked by the doctors, Nick phoned Mike to come and collect us. Fortunately for him, he had had an appointment that morning, and was unavailable for the team meeting. From the office, I drove my car home, swallowed two paracetamol tablets, and went to bed.

The following Monday morning, all accident victims were called to the office to discuss the insurance aspect of the incident. By then, my injuries had set-in, and the pain I was feeling in my neck and shoulders was excruciating. 10 out of 10 on the pain-o-meter!

"I don't want you claiming from my workers compensation insurance," Nick announced, "any medical expenses incurred can be claimed through the Motor Vehicle Insurance Office. It wasn't my fault, and I'll sue the driver of the other car. Here is the claim number. Ensure you use it when receiving treatment for all injuries incurred on Friday."

This meant I still had to work, even though I was finding it nigh on impossible due to the pain. Fear set in as I contemplated my future. The medical diagnosis: whiplash. The prognosis was pain, which could last for years, so just deal with it.

I forced myself to carry on working as before but found the discomfort debilitating. As I drove buyers around in my car to view homes, I omitted to tell them about my severe agony. I failed to mention I couldn't even lift my head to see out of the rear-view mirror, or even move my neck to look at the side mirrors. I certainly did not tell them I was drugged up with Panadol Forte. Every action was painful. I called on my family for all hands-on deck.

Erica would hold my shopping bag, pack the groceries, and even fill out the signed cheques to pay for our purchases. By the end stage of the shop, I needed to head for the nearest bench seat to rest. Glen took over the cooking responsibilities, Erica the washing, and Ray the vacuuming. I could no longer hold Alice, not that I was ever able to get close to her, but I did need to grab her hand from time to time, to prevent her from dashing off in all directions. I could no longer enjoy even personal aspects of my life. Every movement had a reactive *"Ouch!"*

Real estate sales were becoming a scarcity. With caring for Alice, physiotherapy appointments, forcing myself to drive the short distance to my office to complete basic tasks, and sleeping, there was no time or energy left for work.

Linda would often come to my house where we'd both curl up on the lounge and nurse our injuries to the cries of oohs, aahs and ouches with every move we made.

Life wasn't supposed to be like this. I had goal set. Until this time, my life was going to plan. We had purchased a bigger, newer home with all the bells and whistles in Bateman. Alice had started kindergarten nearby. Glen had completed his high schooling (no, he wasn't a great scholar, just a great person), and started working under Ray at Furniture Hire. Erica was attending Rossmoyne High School, was in the State Volleyball Team, and excelled at Little Athletics. Hooray! We were supposed to be enjoying the good life! The car crash was not on my agenda!

Three years later I was awarded a payout for my injuries, which cleared our debts. The financial pressure was finally off me. However, the physical pain endured. Real estate was never to be the same again.

I was fast losing my passion for sales. Fortunately, Ray was now the main breadwinner, and that suited me fine. I was sick of selling myself to prospective clients, and was finally doing some fun activities, like not taking work so seriously.

As the years rolled on, I half-heartedly continued to carry out the motions of the job, because I loved working with my two buddies. Mike, renowned as a good operator by his industry peers, went on to start his own real estate agency, and his fortunes grew. Whenever I had suggested that it was time for me to move on to find another job, I had allowed him and Linda to talk me out of it. Anyway, what else could I do? I didn't have any other skills. All I could do was talk to people. I couldn't even type.

Then, one day, completely unexpectedly, for me anyway, I discovered Mike and Linda had partnered up and were planning to leave their respective spouses. Well, I hadn't seen that one coming! They hadn't even had the courage to tell me. I had suspected nothing! I felt like a complete fool. There we had been, playing happy families and now I learnt we'd all been living a lie. I told myself it was not my husband who was leaving me. Why then had I taken this news so badly?

Marriage break-ups had been unfamiliar territory for me. I was still under the assumption that "what God has put together, let no man put asunder." Had I not gone through thick and thin myself, and still managed to protect my husband and children from this sort of pain? Although the three of us had confided in each other about our personal problems, I couldn't believe they would ever have the audacity, or was it the courage, to do that. What had happened to "until death do us part, for better or for worse, for richer, for poorer etc?" Just a year earlier Mike had told me that he had had romantic feelings towards me. I also felt close to him and had valued our special friendship. However, for the sakes of our spouses and children, we agreed to put these feelings aside and just remain friends.

I couldn't face them any longer. What right did they have to seek happiness together? I hadn't even detected that they had a romantic attraction to each other.

Were my feelings those of anger or abandonment? Was I jealous they had found love with each other? Did I feel sorry for their spouses and six children? Had I not promised Mike's extremely insecure wife I would not do anything to ruin her family? I couldn't be a party to this new situation. I'd promised! Was I judging them according to my own old-fashioned values? Would my relationship with both parties and their respective families change? Yes, to all the above! Would I have done the same thing myself if it was on offer to me? No! I had far too many responsibilities of my own at home.

***

When I walked into my office the following day, Sunday, I felt an overwhelming feeling of spiritual heaviness hit me like a load of bricks. I fell to the floor and sobbed my heart out. *I can't do this anymore. I've got to get out of here. I feel suffocated!* I drove home, swallowed two sleeping pills, and went to bed. I never did go back to that office. My ten years of real estate sales had ended.

Goodbye real estate. I'd like to say it was fun while it lasted but I cannot lie!

***

It wasn't until three years later that I felt strong enough, or was that forgiving enough, to speak to Linda again. By then I understood that this was their destiny. Together they'd faced the trials of their own marriage breakdowns. Linda embraced Mike's four children, and together they built a large home to accommodate their blended family of eight. I respect Linda and Mike for their dedication to their family and to each other.

They've now been married for over 25 years and have 12 grandchildren. I still catch up with them from time to time.

Chapter 25

I'm As Clever As Anyone

During three months of self-imposed home detention, I had taken time out to address my anger and grief issues. I eventually concluded I'd become co-dependent on my friends. I'd had them on a pedestal as being all I wanted to aspire to. The time had come for me to set them free from my mind, learn new skills, and stand on my own two feet. They had their chosen destiny, and now I must choose mine. Ray had been extremely patient and encouraged me to take as much time as I needed to work through my emotions. It was time to go out to face the world again. *But where do I begin? I think I'll start with the Commonwealth Employment Bureau in Fremantle.*

"Are you looking for a job?" asked a kind middle-aged lady.

"Yes, I am, but I can't see anything on this list I could see myself doing," I replied.

"I think you're in the wrong place. These jobs are for labouring positions. Just looking at you, I think you'd be successful in a public relations type job."

Oh, my goodness, that Public Relations word again!

"How do you get into that?"

"Well, you do need to be qualified to get a job in that field. I suggest you go up to Perth, to the Albert Facey Centre, and find out who's running a course."

"Thank you, you have been extremely helpful. Are you the careers adviser here?"

"No," she laughed, "I'm here searching for a job for myself."

However, there I was, driving to Perth, thanks to the advice of the angel I had met just 15 minutes ago.

On arrival at the Albert Facey Centre, I asked the receptionist about Public Relations courses, and she mentioned there'd be one commencing at Perth Central TAFE the following semester. She recommended I walk over to the PCT building nearby and speak with one of the lecturers. Once again, no-one had to tell me twice. Within minutes I was sitting before the lecturer in charge of the PR Course.

"You do have your TEE?" he asked. The Tertiary Entrance Examination. Entry to higher education can only be gained with this qualification.

"No," I answered. I had bailed from school after year 11, with a back injury, the result of a horse-riding accident. I couldn't face walking, carrying a heavy school bag, the five kilometres to and from school every day. When I mentioned the possibility of leaving school to my mother, her only words were "Just, make sure you get a job first." The following day, I walked into the R&I Bank, wearing my school uniform, and applied for a job. My sister Anne had worked in that bank before her marriage and was well thought of by the Bank Manager. I was *a shoo-in*. I became the only female R&I Bank employee ever who couldn't type.

"Well, you will have to sit the TISC Exam (Tertiary Institution Service Centre) then," advised the lecturer.

"Okay, how does one do that?"

"You go to the TISC office at the University of Western Australia, Office for Adult University Entrance, and you apply," he replied in what I perceived as an arrogant manner. *Like I was supposed to know this stuff, or maybe, I was going to have to tone down my exuberance… again.*

"Once you have your results, come back here, and apply for the Public Relations Course. Oh, and this PR course will be a special elite course, so we will be very selective in our candidates. Just don't take it as a given that you will be accepted, even if you do eventually have the credentials to apply."

I had never let an egotistical male deter me in the past, and I was not about to let one get the better of me now. I went straight back to my car and headed off to the University of Western Australia to register for the English and Humanities TISC exams. I was advised that high scores in these subjects would assure me a place in the PR course and could also earn me a place in nursing and teaching at university. Too easy, or so I thought!

On the day of the first exam, Humanities, I was feeling most apprehensive as I entered the exam hall. Everyone appeared so friendly, and most of the students already knew each other.

"I don't remember you from the course," commented a young lady as she acknowledged my nervous smile."

"Course? What course?"

I soon learned there had been a lengthy course which had prepared these students for the TISC exams. Well, nobody had told me about that one! I had arrived for the exam without having done the course. *I'm just going to have to do my best. Perhaps I can do the required course if this day turns to mush.*

For four hours, I worked my way through the exam questions. *Gees, I've got no idea how I'm going, but I'll keep at it anyway, I've paid good money to be here.* Several of the bright student finished early, got up, handed in their papers, and left. At that point, I wasn't even halfway through.

"Right, time's up, pens down," ordered the supervisor. *That had to be the worst four hours of my life.* I literally ran back to my car, locked myself in, and cried. I vowed not to tell a soul I had even attempted the exam.

The prospect of failure was looming! I resolved to wait for the results before deciding whether to sit the English exam. It cost money to sit for the exams, and I couldn't afford to waste our resources on a doomed mission. Within a few weeks, I received an official looking envelope in the mail. Nervously, I sneaked away to open it. Well*, here goes, fingers crossed.* My result read 165 out of 200 which was above average. I was in total shock! *Okay then, back for the next one.*

I enjoyed the English exam, which involved writing, writing, and more writing on a variety of subjects for four hours solid. My English results were 188 out of 200, which was spectacular. Well, I thought so!

I immediately contacted the TAFE lecturer to inform him of my TISC results.

"Hi, its Karin. I passed the TISC exam with above average results. What do I do now? I was so excited. That old exuberance was resurfacing, yet again.

"Oh, umm, now I want you to write a formal application, stating why you believe you should be selected for the Public Relations Course. I also need three formal references from citizens of good repute, stating why they believe you would make a suitable candidate for………. *Prime Minister?" No, for TAFE!*

The following week, with my beautifully bound, formal documentation in place, I proudly marched into the TAFE office, and handed in my mega file application.

I soon discovered the PR course applicants were judged on a point system, with 40 being the highest points possible. A score under 30 would render one ineligible for acceptance. At the commencement of the first semester, I learnt I was the only student who received the full 40 points. The second nearest score was 36 points. That very lecturer, who had initially made my application so difficult, was a hard taskmaster, and a very gifted lecturer who knew how to get the best out of the students who genuinely wanted to succeed.

Have you ever felt like you just want to run out the door and hide? I felt that way during my first computer lesson which I found to be excruciatingly complicated. First you turn on the power at the wall, which I labelled with a sticky note, on which I wrote the number one. Then I labelled the computer box thingo as number two. Finally, the button that you turn on the keyboard thingy, I labelled…. you guessed it, number three. So much to remember!

"Okay, type in your name," instructed the lecturer, once she was confident all students had mastered the art of switching on a computer. *My goodness, where is that letter K, and God only knows where that R is hiding. Gees, typing is so tricky!*

During my high school years, typing lessons had not been an option for me. I was earmarked as an academic, and supposedly didn't need to learn that lowly skill. As a would-be, could-be, should-be professional, I'd have people doing my typing for me. In hindsight, I realise typing would have been a far handier workplace ability than speaking French and German, my chosen subjects at the time which, I might add, were never called upon during my banking or real estate careers.

As days turned into weeks and weeks into months, I mastered the computer, and became competent at using the Office 95 suite. I enjoyed Publisher and loved to enhance my assignments with an artistically designed cover. Not that that was appreciated by the lecturers. They weren't looking for fancy. They wanted content. However, I gave great content plus great fancy!

I learnt the intricacies of the three forms of Public Relations: not for profit, business promotions, and utilising PR for everyday business. I studied the difference between marketing a product and marketing a service. My right brain personality tolerated Business Law, Statistics, and Business Accounting, but thrived at Letter Writing, Publication Writing, and Report Writing.

All the students in that group were aged in their twenties or thirties, or so they thought.

"You're in your thirties, aren't you? asked a 24-year-old classmate. *Flattery will get you everywhere!*

"Yep, I'm thirty-twelve," I conceded. From that exercise, I discovered I was the eldest in the group, but I didn't let that deter me. Once again, I was on a mission to become employable. I soon learnt that I was just as clever as anyone who worked their proverbial butt off. I became obsessed with my studies and devoted every waking hour to my learning and presentation techniques. Once again, my desire to prove myself as worthy overpowered all I did. One day I had only received 95% for a marketing assignment and asked to see the lecturer in private.

"Can you please tell me what I could have done to attain a higher score? I queried.

"I appreciate your question, but I'm here to tell you: no one is perfect, and everyone has room for improvement," he patiently explained. *Oh well, at least I now know!*

By the end of 1996, I had my Advanced Certificate of Public Relations in my hot little hand. Just six students graduated from that *elite* course. The remaining 14 had dropped out over the year, as they'd found the workload to be far too demanding. Really? Not that I cared. I'd learnt a plethora of new transferable skills, and now considered myself to be employable. Someone out there was going to pay me to work for them. I would no longer need to work on a commission-only basis.

Chapter 26

Men With Feet Of Clay

"You need healing," said Rose, the physiotherapist, as she expertly massaged the tightened muscles in my neck and upper back.

I lay on the physiotherapists table in tears. The chronic pain of my whiplash injury, sustained in the car accident several years earlier, was still excruciating but that was not all. Not only was I crying about my physical pain, I was also crying about my emotional pain. My life was not supposed to be regressing. I was supposed to be going forward. My goals to date had brought us to a place where we were finding financial independence, our children were thriving, the older two kids were totally independent, and the little one, was, let me just say, contained. The world was supposed to be my oyster, but that was before the car accident.

I had never experienced constant severe physical pain before, the type that went on for day after day with no reprieve. I was at the point where I had no enthusiasm or energy for my job as a real estate salesperson and at that time had taken a hiatus from real estate to sort out my mind, body, and soul. I discovered every muscle in my body was somehow connected to my neck and back, as I hurt with every task, whether it be holding my child, carrying a handbag, driving my car, walking, or even sleeping. I was also still suffering the emotional pain of my experience with James. Life became one long moment of pain, and there, on the physiotherapists table, through my tears, I told Rose why I was crying.

"Yes, you do need healing. Are you free next Wednesday afternoon? I would like you to come to The City Church and have healing prayers said for you."

Is this another angel pointing the way for me, I thought? *If so, I will not dismiss it as a pile of mumbo jumbo. I so desperately need help. I can't take this pain anymore.*

Churches were not fresh territory for me. I had spent my girlhood as a Lutheran, where I learnt all about the wrath of God. I learnt I was not worthy so much as to gather up the crumbs under Jesus's table. I learnt

I was a miserable sinner and needed to repent to have everlasting life. If not, I would be delivered into an afterlife of hellfire and brimstone.

Once married, and with true black sheep bravado, I attended the Anglican Church, where I learnt a whole new concept of religion: God is Love. How truly shocked was I? The word love had never been mentioned in the church just up the road. If it was, I must have been recoiling in the corner as all I recalled was a vengeful God. Good-will towards mankind was taught. Wow, now that was a revelation!

Once I moved to Perth, the principal of my company invited me to attend his church. Here I learnt that even Baptists drink alcohol, but not when any of the congregation can see them. Funnily enough, they did plenty of other stuff, also not where the congregation could see them. However, Ray, our children, and I threw ourselves into community life and, strangely enough, often felt like we were left holding the baby when it came to fundraisers and busy bees, as most of the congregation were elderly and unable to contribute physically.

We had been warned about Pentecostal churches. Happy clappy, they called them, where they have people speaking in tongues and worshipping devilish spirits. Unperturbed by gossip and innuendo, I wasn't going to let others stop me from being healed, if that was at all possible. I'd had enough of physical pain. I'd also had enough of emotional pain. I was ready for a miracle.

The following Wednesday I lined up for prayer at the City Church. Rose, physiotherapist, and lead singer in the church band, was by my side encouraging me to let go of my emotions, and to hand my pain over to God. The Pastor came over to me, touched my neck and prayed. Instantly, I found myself on the floor sobbing my heart out. And, what's more, my pain had eased.

Back at home I told Ray about the healing session, and asked if I could go to their Sunday Service. He offered to come with me. Here began a very fulfilling relationship with the supernatural and their enthusiastic followers. The congregation was a lively bunch, and openly displayed their love for God, Jesus, and the Holy Spirit. The auditorium pounded with the banging of drums, twanging of guitars, and singers belting out their songs of praise with gusto.

With each healing session came more pain relief. I was hooked. I also became addicted to learning scripture. I was on a mission to learn as much as I could about God and his word. Ray and I also thought that if I could be healed, perhaps Alice could also be healed of her behavioural problems, which were nameless at the time. We mentioned this to Alice who, although only six years old, rebelled even further.

She'd make every effort to not accompany Ray and me on our Sunday pilgrimage, hiding in her wardrobe or under the bed, refusing to get dressed, and screaming until we gave up and left her home with her siblings. When I did manage to coax her into the car one day, she refused get out, and would run from lock to lock, shutting them as we raced around the outside of the vehicle, trying to outsmart her.

The one time we did succeed in dragging her up for prayer, she screamed, kicked, and bit the Pastor. She wasn't having any of that spiritual stuff! I was also surprised at her attitude towards Sunday School. Where all the other little kids would happily listen to the biblical stories and sing "Jesus Loves Me," Alice spent the entire hour plotting her escape from the room. When asked how her Sunday School went, she said,

"It was shit and I'm not singing those stupid songs." *My goodness, did she need healing or what*!

My thirst for all things scriptural grew, and each Sunday I'd sit in the congregation with Bible and yellow marker in hand, eagerly highlighting the passages and verses which spoke to me. In no time my bible had the look of being trashed with dog ears, graffiti, and coloured-in to the max. It appeared old, used, torn and tattered. I loved it.

Within no time, Ray and I were part of the social group at the church and would often lend a hand where required at busy bees, street marches, and catering. We even invited strangers who I judged as needing hospitality, to our home for a meal, friendship, and/or my designer clothes hand-me-downs.

"Will you organise my wedding reception?" asked Jean, the Pastor's fiancée who I saw as a total sweetheart with a heart of pure gold.

"I'd love to," I answered, not even knowing what really was being asked of me. "Thank you. I'd be honoured. How many guests will you be having?" I asked as I immediately swung into Miss Organising mode.

"About 400 hundred." she replied.

My head spun but I didn't want to give her the impression that I was incompetent and calmly said:

"Oh, okay." I was left wondering what 400 people in one room would even look like.

There is nothing like getting an insight into a congregation when you ask them to give or do something beyond the realm of spiritual gifting. For so long, I'd believed they were all holier than me, and I respected them for it. I even envied them. God's chosen ones who could speak in tongues, sing beautifully, play a musical instrument, channel the Holy Spirit, had been personally visited by Jesus himself, and vowed true love and allegiance to the Pastor and his fiancée.

Well, you should have seen them head for the hills when I asked them to make a savoury dish, set up tables, or help Ray and me organise the wedding. Suddenly, that was not their calling or their gifting, they had hair appointments, or just couldn't be available at any of the busy bee times. They would, however, be at the church to see their beloved Pastor wed and would attend the reception as a guest.

"So, make sure you set a place for me," many said.

Fortunately, much of the preparation had been done in the weeks before. I had baked the 1600 profiteroles in my home oven. One of the ladies had made beautiful floral arrangements for the tables. The cutlery, plates, and table clothes were hired and transported in by Ray. The main meal had been cooked offsite and was to be brought in by the butcher and his team. The young girls wore matching waitress uniforms which had been specially made by a small team of seamstresses. For days, Alice and I had wrapped chocolates in cellophane, and tied them up with ribbon.

Alice was a tremendous help to me as she counted the chocolates into piles, or so I thought. I was soon to discover it was one for the pile, one for Alice, one for the pile, one for Alice. Yes, helpful indeed! History also repeated itself when I called on my youngest child to help me fold 400 serviettes into a fancy design. A task Glen and Erica had assisted me with for my fundraisers, on so many occasions all those years ago.

With limited assistance on the day of the wedding, Ray and I spent the morning setting up and dressing the tables at the venue, the Melville Hall. The entire afternoon was taken up with whipping up copious quantities of cream and filling 1600 profiteroles, arranging them onto plates and drizzling each with chocolate.

We were the only members of the congregation who did not attend the wedding ceremony or sit down for the entire night. Thankfully, a small group volunteered to stay behind to help us clean the premises, and by 3.00am Ray and I headed home for a well-earned rest.

Oh well, another study in human nature! Even self-proclaimed godly people were human, it seemed. In fact, they were no different to any other group I'd ever belonged to, religious or not. I suppose it was me who'd put them on a pedestal and watched them all fall, one after another, like a succession of dominoes. Yes, they were "men of feet of clay," just like me![4]

As the days and weeks went on, I found it harder and harder to remain enthused about this spiritually gifted group of human beings. After their shirking of responsibility at the wedding, I was slowly working out that these people and I had absolutely nothing in common. Their public persona was that the holy spirit shone exclusively on them, but as soon as they were asked to contribute, they suddenly turned all human. Before long, it became impossible for me to even want to open my Bible or highlight a word, let alone a full verse. I sat in the congregation feeling nothing but cold, disillusioned, and conned. *Time to go Karin!*

---

[4] *The Bible*, Book of Daniel: Men of Clay Feet: referring to human weakness or character flaws.

Chapter 27

Out Of The Wilderness

"Is that Karin?" asked a gentle sounding male voice over the phone.

I acknowledged my name, hoping to goodness I wasn't going to get conned into buying yet another product I didn't need. Being a salesperson myself, I had empathy with all cold canvassers, as so many times in my real estate career, that enquiring, gentle voice at the other end of the phone was mine.

"Can I help you?" I replied. For the 10 years of my real estate sales career, I'd lived in the hope that every phone call could be a lead to a house listing or a sale, hence my much practised, pleasant demeanour. However, real estate was my past life. I was now a Public Relations Student.

"My name is Robert, and I am the Pastor at the Local Pentecostal Church. I was given your name by a mutual friend, and thought I'd phone to inquire where you are at in your spiritual journey."

"Well, I'm not exactly on a spiritual journey. In fact, I got off the spiritual train a while ago. I worked it out that churches are full of human beings, no better or worse than any other people in the world. I also worked out that God, whoever that may be, doesn't necessarily live in churches, and he, if it's he at all, is not Father Christmas in the sky judging me as naughty or nice, and rewarding me accordingly.

"Thought-provoking observation! They're my sentiments exactly. You sound like a remarkably interesting person." With that we segued into a conversation lasting over an hour, as we discussed our own perceived truths in relation to religion. Although I had never met him, our conversation was unrestrained, comfortable, and intelligent. *Most interesting! I love a decent conversation about issues which are close to my heart. I think I'll pop in on Sunday to see what's so special about his church.*

The church was intimate, just 30 people in the rented hall. Robert, the pastor, a man in his early fifties, appeared to have the congregation holding onto his every word and gesture. At the keyboard stood a tall, well dressed, striking looking woman. She beamed a radiant smile at me as I sat down. I soon learnt she was his wife. There was happy clapping singing, spiritual healing at the altar, a short sermon which spoke to my heart, and some very friendly people around me, all of whom made me feel very welcome.

"Ray, I think I'll go again," I announced to my easy-going yet tolerant husband.

"I'll come with you," he promptly replied. He sounded surprisingly keen, but I soon realised my vigilant husband had volunteered his services purely as my bodyguard. He knew me well and wanted to be there to rein in my passions, my enthusiasm, and my vulnerabilities. He had witnessed it all before and knew that I would absolutely crash again.

Well, there we went once more, headfirst into a life of bible study, church services and fellowship. Ray was well accepted, everyone appeared to love him. I was left standing on the outer, wishing I had a friendly demeanour just like him. I could only surmise that my well-groomed appearance and designer clothes may have put many people off. They were clearly dressed for comfort, not glamour. I personally didn't see it as a barrier, but soon heard, through the grapevine, that my dress sense had made some people feel uncomfortable with me. However, this was my look. This was the way I dressed seven days a week. I didn't have any other clothes and I certainly didn't own jeans and sweat tops. They are so not me!

Once again, Ray and I were thrust into a small community, and a hectic social life ensued. We were invited out to dinners, picnics, and concerts. Ray was even elected to the Church Board, a position he reluctantly accepted. He often wondered why the members were making such a big song and dance about issues which could have been so easily resolved if they stopped talking and just acted.

"The meetings are just total bullshit," he'd say. "Talk about a waste of time, they carry on as though they are running the country, not a tin pot church." Ray was a practical man. No talk, and all action.

Being such a small congregation, I was given many opportunities to have my moment in the sun. I was asked to write short sermons, and to give the address. I loved it. I was given a computer program which contained five versions of the bible, and I'd spend my week writing a sermon using all five adaptations as my points of reference. I thrived! I was so happy! I felt truly alive!

I was also asked to write a Passion Play, and to produce it. The opportunity to work with the congregation and the musicians will always be a bittersweet memory for me. Why bittersweet? The sweet bit was having the competence and the ability to write the play and to produce it. The bitter aspect were the jealousies and judgements that surfaced thereafter.

In life, I have found, you can have talent, but please be average. One should look average, aspire to average, and achieve average. That way everyone feels good about themselves. Especially the average ones. Once again, my enthusiasm and passion for life was causing divide. I had come to be held in high regard by the Pastor, who gave me every opportunity to use my God given talents to bless the flock. We became close friends, yes, perhaps too close. This connection caused upset, not only in the congregation but also with his wife. Was this becoming a familiar pattern for me?

For everyone's benefit, Ray and I felt it would be wise for us to graciously exit that group. History was repeating itself as I realised again that humans are humans. They weren't Jesus, no matter how hard they worked to be Christlike. Yes, these folks were also "men with feet of clay," just like me! Bless 'em!

Did I go back into the wilderness? No, I went back to a place of clarity and peace, where Ray and I worked out if it was going to be, it was up to us to join forces and live our own dreams. I had my guardian angels, but that, I believed, was subjective. It worked for me, and if others did not agree, then they must find their own truths.

Chapter 28

The Pollyanna Dream

"Have I got a job for you!" Kathy, my employment agent, yelled down the phone. Yes, *my* Employment Agent! Everyone who is employable has a personal employment agent. And I was uber employable … now!

***

After a year of full-time Public Relations studies, I'd gained a certificate in must-have skills that, all things going well, should make me a qualified candidate for most office jobs. But did I really want to sit in an office from nine to five and take orders? I was so used to coming and going as I pleased. In sales, I was the master of my own destiny, had created my own good and/or bad fortunes, was used to relying on my own creativity and my own skills at relationship building.

I did not mind working on the weekends or receiving phone calls at all hours of the night. I had always been prepared to make a job my own, to take charge and to make it happen. The thought of being an easily replaceable cog in a big wheel somehow did not sit well with me.

After much deliberation I decided, I did not want to lose my real estate sales license. The licensing course was now a four-week event, and the cost had risen to well over a thousand dollars. And what is more, I loved the real-estate industry. It had already given me so many opportunities for personal growth and financial success.

I suddenly had a vision of doing property management, but with flair. Most property managers I had met in my selling days were frazzled, peeved-off ladies who appeared to hate their clients. Dealing with them, I had often wondered if there could be a better method of doing that job. Now I was devising a plan of using my own people loving skills to build good public relations between management, tenants, and owners. I began having dreams, or were they hallucinations, of using my new-found creative PR skills to build and manage the best asset management portfolio in town.

But first, I needed to be accepted for a placement in the management industry. I already had ten years of honest, no nonsense business relationships with many of the representatives and local agents within 15 kilometres of my home. My first job application was as personal assistant to the principal of a small, family-run rental management business. He immediately employed me without me having had any prior property management experience. That company dealt only in executive properties in the riverside suburbs of Applecross and surrounds. I soon learnt the intricacies of the now superseded DOS computer program, along with the pressures of the job. The principal was a particularly gruelling task master, often to the point of pedantic. However, I appreciated the opportunity to learn under his finicky control. I believed I was learning to do the job right the first time, something I did eventually become thankful for.

Within 18 months, I was head-hunted by a renowned Applecross real estate agent in need of a property manager with sales experience to build their company a rent roll from scratch. To me, this sounded like the ideal job. A job where I could design, create, and fulfil my Pollyanna dream of making everyone happy.

On my first day with the new company, I was shown my very own office. Okay, it was a small, partitioned area, containing an old fashion wooden desk, a rickety office chair, and an empty scratched metal filing cabinet. It was virtually:

"Well, there's your office. Off you go, knock yourself out and build us a rent roll."

As I waited for a computer and a phone to be installed, I busied myself by ordering the prescribed property management forms and documentation. I was given a free hand in designing the Property Management (PM) Handbook, so I set about this task, applying my newly acquired Window 95 Publisher skills from my PR course. I called on knowledge from my previous rental management employment and the Property Management Qualification Course. I also utilised my selling skills, enhanced in my real estate sales days. In hindsight, nobody ever cared or even questioned what I was doing in my little cubicle until the last day of the month, when my profit and loss figures were sought. Fortunately, these improved monthly.

I was in seventh heaven as I visited prospective clients, sold my management capability, designed our company propaganda (advertising material), and enlisted their properties for my well-respected employers. However, building great relationships with the owners was one thing, while managing even the wealthiest of tenants was a separate issue altogether. Every tenant believed themselves to be experts in the Residential Tenancy Act, thinking they knew more than me. Preposterous! I soon began to understand why property managers always appeared frazzled. Despite my absolute best intentions to keep all parties happy, I could only do my job, according to law, without fear or favour.

Within two years, the rent-roll had grown to a two-person job. I had given the company my absolute best but had come to the realisation that I didn't enjoy being a Property Manager anymore. It was far too stressful! I am sorry for judging you Property Managers out there and yes, I can understand why wine is a necessary commodity in the industry.

***

However, I loved building rent-rolls, and let Kathy know of my passion.

"Okay, what's the job, Kathy," I asked.

"It's called a Business Development Manager. There's a city-based company, recently floated on the stock exchange, and they're looking for someone to organically grow their rent-roll. You wouldn't have to manage the properties, just source them."

"Do you really think I could do that? I've never heard of that position before."

"You'd be perfect for the job, and they are going to love you. I'll set up the appointment for an interview." After a short process of separate interviews with all business partners, I was given the job to be the first, or at least one of the first, Business Development Managers in Western Australia.

No-one, not even the office manager, knew what my job involved, so I was given carte blanche to do my own thing. I thrived. Once again, I used my marketing, Publisher, Excel, and most of my public relations and sales skills, acquired along the way, to just get out and do what was required of me, which was to list rental properties for our property management team to manage. I was flying high and loving each day.

"We'd like to clone you," remarked one of the managers, as he was perusing my monthly achievement reports. They would often show their appreciation for my efforts by giving me pay rises, gift cards, meals out, and invitations to networking functions.

When that company was sold off, a few years later, I chose not to go with the new owners. I jumped back on the phone to Kathy, and she came up with an even bigger and better deal. When one has an employment agent, one has the luxury to chop and change jobs as one's mood dictates. For the next few years, I worked in several renowned metropolitan rental management companies as their Business Development Manager, a job tailor-made just for me.

In Memory of Kathy Dunlop 1953-2020

Chapter 29

A Mother's Fear

"Glen, you awake. Where's Erica?" I whispered, as I crept into his darkened room.

"I don't know. We came home from the night club a while ago," he drowsily answered.

"She's not in her room. I thought I heard a car driving off ten minutes ago, but I was hoping it was the neighbour's and not hers."

"She didn't tell me she was going anywhere. But she did ask if I wanted to go to Metropolis Nightclub in Fremantle. I told her I was too tired. She didn't say she was going on her own!" said Glen as he sat bolt upright, now fully awake. It was the early hours of a Saturday morning, and I could not find my 18-year-old daughter. She was supposed to be in her bed. She didn't mention to me she would be going out again. She had usually let me know of her movements, if I was lucky.

She was impromptu in her desires, her outings, and with her social calendar. Many an evening I would be home waiting for her return, her dinner in the oven, pacing the floor, peering behind the curtains to see if she was coming up the road. I allowed her to go out at night. She was not a prisoner, but I tried to impart to our two older kids that we were a family, and nine-year-old Alice still required a family routine. She didn't need for her older siblings to be using the house like a hotel, coming, and going, making noises at all hours, and not informing us of their whereabouts.

I went back to bed and woke Ray.

"Ray, I'm worried. Erica's gone out and I don't know where she is."

"She'll be back soon," he replied, fully confident his eldest daughter was in no harm, driving around the metropolitan area at 1.00am in the morning to a destination unknown. "Go back to sleep," he grumbled.

"Well, you may be able to sleep, but I can't." So typical: sleep appeared more important to him than the welfare of our highly spirited, vivacious, voluptuous, blond bombshell of a daughter? It was usually okay with me if she was out with Glen. He didn't drink alcohol, and I trusted him to taxi Erica about, but I knew Erica liked to drink her fair share, even at that age.

Lying on my bed, I tried to relax, but sleep did not come. Every time I heard a vehicle pass our house; I jumped up to see if I could see her car in the driveway. Hours went by. I still couldn't find the peace to sleep.

I glanced over at the electric clock on Ray's bedside table. It read 4.00am.

"Right, that's it," I shrieked, as I jumped out of bed and began pulling on my tracksuit.

"Ray if you don't do something, I bloody well will. It's likely she's gone to Metros in Fremantle. She should have been home by now. If something has happened to her, I could never live with myself. Why aren't you worried? So typical: sleep is more important than your daughter," I bitterly accused. Ray, by then sick of my fish wife antics, crawled out of bed, went into the walk-in robe, found his white shirt and blue slacks, and got dressed. *That's appropriate, his nightclub attire.*

"I'll go and find her," he finally conceded. "Are you coming?" I sure was! I was not going to lay about while my beautiful little big girl was God knows where. Driving the 11 kilometres to Fremantle, nothing was said. My mind was going crazy with worry, as I thought of at least a hundred worst case scenarios.

At that time of morning, there were many free parking bays right outside the Metropolis Nightclub's front door. *Of course, there are. Anyone in their right mind would be home in bed, wouldn't they?*

Ray, dressed in his smart clubbing gear, got out of the car, and walked over to speak to the burly bouncer who was still guarding the entry. I stayed in the car, as I was inappropriately dressed in just a tracksuit.

"Would Erica Jarvis please report to the front door. Your father is here to pick you up," requested the DJ over the night club's public address system.

Erica, who was in the building happily chatting to her new-found friends, heard her name being publicly called out, and raced towards the door, shaking her head in absolute horror. When she caught Ray's eyes, she shot him a look of utter disdain. He said nothing and pointed to the door. She'd got the message, grabbed her bag, and headed out down the road towards her car.

We followed her vehicle home. I was ready for a fight. Ray suggested we leave it until morning as we'd wake up the other kids. Did I listen to Ray? No!

"Sit down young lady." I ordered. Before I had a chance to explain how worried I had been for the last four hours, she glared at us, and flames of anger shot from her eyes as she screamed.

"You two are the most embarrassing people I know. Nobody's parents have ever done that before! I'll never be able to hold my head up high in that place again. Everybody was laughing at me as I left the night club."

"I've been worried sick. I couldn't sleep all night wondering where you were." She rolled her eyes and shot me a glare of hate. I fought back my emotions, as I really felt like giving her soiled makeup and tear sodden face a bloody good slap.

"Just a minute my girl, if you live in this house, you have to abide by the family rules," I responded in an equally over-reactive manner.

"Well, I won't live here then," she screamed back. "I'm sick of living here. I get stuck with Alice all day long. I can't have friends over because Alice interrupts us all the time. Mum, living here is shit! You're never home! You can watch after your own bloody kid! I'm done!"

Well, that went well. What was I supposed to do? I was so relieved to have her home in one piece. Didn't she understand? I was tired. I had to work. Nobody had ever given me anything. And stuck with Alice? I was often thankful that she was stuck with Alice, as at least that made my free-spirited elder daughter responsible, and ensured she would at least be home on time, even if only to fulfil her Alice obligations. She is 18. God knows I was married at that age, and running my own life, although not well, and certainly not in accordance with my dreams. That's right: I didn't have any dreams. Oh, the nurse thing? Yeah, we all know what happened there! I must allow Erica to dream, to find herself, to become. I can't keep her caged any longer. I'm going to have to trust in a higher power. I have done all I can.

The following day I found my teenage daughter armed with a red pen, going through the "Rooms to Let" section of the newspaper, making her intentions clear by placing red circles around possible leads. A room! One room! Here, at our house, she had her own room, several rooms with TVs, a pool, a secure place to park her car, meals placed on the table every night, clean laundry twice a week, no bills to pay, a dad to fix stuff, and a mum to rescue her physically and financially at the drop of a hat. I understood she loved her golf, rowing, bike riding, parties, nightclubbing, and buying clothes, but why does she want to move out? *Go where you like, my love, but please just tell me. Easily fixed!*

Erica had left school at the age of sixteen and a half and had immediately found full-time employment in an accountant's office. She had always had work of some nature, even as a young teenager: delivering milk, letterbox dropping, anything to supplement her busy lifestyle. She had inherited the family manic work ethic and could lay her hand to anything. We were immensely proud of her, and so relieved she hadn't carried the family learning disability gene, like her two siblings.

But her living in one room among a house full of strangers scared me. I could not imagine her existing like that. I was fully aware I had placed a heavy responsibility on her young shoulders by relying on her to care for Alice when I was working. A job she did well, but secretly begrudged. I understood her feelings, as her younger sister's behaviour was totally out of control, but no-one, not even the professionals, had any answers. God knows we had tried so hard to seek help for her!

Ray and I called a meeting with Glen and Erica, where we discussed giving them each a deposit to buy their own homes. A small flat or unit sounded like the best solution. We said we would feel more comfortable if they were in their own properties, and not at the mercy of a landlord. *Besides, there'd be nothing more sobering than for Erica to have her own mortgage. By rights, that should curb her tendency to flit about with no responsibilities!*

Two well priced units were found in the same complex near the Royal Fremantle Golf Club in East Fremantle, Erica's regular scene of socialisation and weekend competition.

If you want to keep your children, you must help carry their bags as they move out. A motto I had heard somewhere and was now practising, as I assisted Erica in setting up her own place. I did not let her see me crying, as I sang to myself over and over, "*…for childhood slips, like sand through a sieve. And all at once they're up and grown, and then you know that it's too late for you to give that spoon full of sugar to make the medicine go down, the medicine go down etc.* (Words from a song in the 1964 movie, Mary Poppins, sung by Bert to Mr Banks, when the father realises he has spent too much time at work, and not enough time with his children.)[5]

I helped paint walls, make curtains, and delighted in buying housewares with colour coordinated accessories. Ray installed pictures on the walls, made new cupboard bench tops, and hung window fittings and fixtures. Assisted by Glen, they carried furniture up the three flights of steps to her unit. Carting Erica's possessions: a chore they were to do many, many more times in the years to come.

I was happy for her but felt utterly distraught. In private I would cry. My role as her mother was over. At 39 years, I was now surplus to her requirements. I had missed most of her teenage years. For the past eight years, I'd been so busy working to put a roof over her head that I'd missed the joy of just being her mother. However, I knew if I was to keep Erica's friendship and respect, I had to let her go. She was a free spirit, fiercely independent and extremely competent to plan and conduct her own life. *"How do you keep a wave upon the sand?"* [6]

"Did she settle down?" one may well ask. No, she did not. She continued do her own merry thing with much gusto, energy, and wit, the only difference being I did not have to watch. What I didn't see, I didn't need to worry about. For my own peace of mind, I handed her over to a higher power.

Erica continues to live her life with liveliness and gusto and recalls her years of living in that unit as her *heyday*.

Glen chose to stay living with us, to continue to enjoy the comforts of home while he rented out his unit. A very astute businessman, he knew the value of an investment. That's my boy, he also knew where his bread was buttered.

***

"Hurry Mum, we'll be late."

Erica glanced over to see her tall, stunningly attractive 22-year-old daughter Jade standing before her wearing a black graduation robe trimmed with crimson silk, the colours of the university's business

---

[5] Sherman, Robert B & Richard M Sherman. *"A Spoon Full of Sugar,"* from *Mary Poppins*, 1964

[6] Hammerstein, Oscar and Richard Rogers. *"How Do You Solve a Problem Like Maria?"* from *The Sound of Music*, USA. 1959

faculty. A black mortar hat completed the young graduate's attire. Erica felt the warmth of love and the elation of pride overwhelm her. Tears came. *I wish Zoe was here to see her sister graduate today,* she thought. But Zoe 19, was living her dream, working in the snowfields on the other side of Australia. *You can't keep a free soul caged!* Both her daughters were now standing on the threshold of their own futures.

At the time of writing, it is 25 years, to the day, since Erica left our family home to commence the climb of her own mountains, and to experience the highs and lows of life for herself. She found love, and had two beautiful daughters, her best and most unexpected gifts. She had found the courage to walk away from personal discontentment and had the strength of character to reset her life's course by pursuing innate passions and developing her professional skills. Now, at just 44 years of age, accomplished in Human Resources and Training, Erica became the designer of her own destiny.

Chapter 30

No More Secrets

"Ray, I think we should split up," I announced as we were finishing up dinner one evening.

"Oh, for goodness sake! Why?" came his shocked reply. During our 26 years of marriage, he had become used to me making impromptu announcements relating to some of my researched ideas, and some of my *not-so-well* researched ideas.

"I've always been someone's daughter, someone's wife, and someone's mother, I don't know what it would be like to just be me. I'd like to live alone to see what it would be like." That's it. I'd finally said it. I'd been thinking about making that announcement for at least three days.

"When were you thinking about going?" he asked, as he shook his head in utter disbelief.

"Today!" I blurted.

"Don't be so bloody stupid. You can't just leave because you are having a bad week. But if it's so bad living with me, at least give yourself some time to think about it." Tears arose in his eyes.

That night, in stony silence, we lay in our bed, not sleeping, just thinking. The silence of the night was intermittently broken by Ray's words, "Don't go, we can work it out. Whatever it is, don't go." Finally, dawn arrived. Ray got out of bed to make me my customary cup of tea. As he placed it on my bed-side cupboard, he asked:

"Well, are you still going?"

"I'm not sure. I've been thinking." At this point I felt the rush of fear for the future and guilt of my past overwhelm my emotions and I began to cry.

"The truth is, love, I'm certain that if you really knew me, the real me, you wouldn't want me anyway." Ray stopped in his tracks, and peered into my tired, sad teary eyes and replied.

"Well, if you really knew me, the real me, you wouldn't want me either." *My goodness, what was he saying? Who, then, is the real Ray? Who have I been married to for all these years? I'm sure I know him. He's just not that complicated, not that exciting and not that interesting!*

"Well, who are you then?" I queried, as I made myself comfortable to settle in for a quick tale about an unambitious, quiet country lad who'd always felt inferior to his two older brothers, who'd married me because it was convenient, who'd been loyal and faithful to his family, who's a great dad and a very supportive husband. *Okay, so what's new?*

As Ray spoke, I found it hard to hide my surprise as he laid out before me his life's secrets. It seemed that while I had been running around trying to be all things to all people, he had also experienced challenges of his own. Some were good, and some not so good. He spoke of the situations he had been exposed to which he was not proud to ever speak of, but did, never-the-less, in minute detail. He told me about the immense anger and grief he'd felt when walking off his much-loved farm. He recounted the solace he'd found in the arms of other women as they sought to console him through his heartache. He spoke about the attractions he had felt with work colleagues over the years, and how he'd managed to get through those times emotionally unscathed. He talked and talked while I sat, completely dumbfounded, in total shock.

Wow, where was I when all this important stuff was going on in this dear soul's life? Why hadn't I seen the signs? What more critical issues had I been attending to when my husband needed me? I sat in complete silence as Ray talked about a man I didn't know. Mind you, that stranger did sound rather exciting, interesting, and sought-after.

After several hours, he concluded with the words, "Okay, your turn now." *Well, after that saga, my tale of woe was going to be a quickie!* I told him, in detail, about the price I believed I had paid for starting anew in Perth. I told him about the copious tears I had cried, the anxiety and the shame I had felt. I told him of attractions I had felt with other men. I even told him that I had lied about the price of an expensive dress I had once bought. Yep, all my sins and transgressions over the past 26 years were being laid bare. Nothing had been held back. Absolutely nothing! But, what now?

I didn't leave. Over the following weeks and months, we spent as much time as possible together, in private, digesting the truths we had revealed to each other. We cried, we stamped our feet, we yelled, we screamed, we cried, and cried some more. I found some self-help books that gave us tips on how to re-build our relationship from that point. It was a very raw, honest, and cathartic experience for us both. No more lies, no more secrets! For the sake of our family, we vowed to turn to each other for comfort and advice should we be faced with problems in the future.

From that time on, Ray and I became best friends. We didn't need besties, mates, the church folk, confidantes, or *hangers-on* to interfere in our lives. We concluded that we were two separate people, neither more nor less worthy than the other, walking together through life. We were both human with our own feelings, appetites, thoughts, and emotions. We weren't clones of each other. Both of us had the right to make mistakes.

It was decreed we must now bury our true passions, abandon our dreams, and walk on together for the sake of the family.

Did we just make a pact to go around the *mulberry bush* one more time? Would our personalities, our individual wants, needs or desires miraculously change? How long must it take to become the true individuals we came to Earth to be?

Perhaps we would need a goodbye, before we ever learnt.

Chapter 31

Who Will Help Alice?

"Mum, Jody reckons I'm ADD," announced my 17-year-old daughter Alice. "He said that's why I am having so much trouble concentrating when I am playing the guitar."

Jody and the boys were Alice's band mates. Together they would persevere with their repertoire of songs in true garage band, rock star wanna-be style. Each aspired to be famous Punk Rock/Indi musicians.

"You know what, Alice?" I replied, "I think he could be onto something."

ADD was not talked much about, especially not in relation to girls. You had your good kids in the class, and you had your brat kids. The good kids got to stay in the classroom to learn, and the brat kids, the ones who wouldn't or couldn't concentrate and became disruptive, were kicked out of the room to sit in the corridors during the lessons. Alice was tagged as a brat kid. She was the only girl sitting outside with the naughty boys.

Alice's behavioural issues were long known to me. Her nightly screaming as a baby stretched into her first seven years. It was impossible to get her to sleep at night. Once sleep finally did come in the wee small hours, it was then difficult to wake her in the morning, especially once she had started school. I suppose I should have smelt a rat when she refused to crawl on the floor as a baby. At seven months of age, she rolled over towards a coffee table, pulled herself up and walked over to me. I didn't know whether I was supposed to be proud of her or make her sit back on the floor again. How do you keep a baby on the floor once they have walked?

Her behaviour was totally foreign to me, as she destroyed every toy, every book, every wall, and every item of furnishing around her. Her bedroom and her play areas resembled a trash heap. I would ask her to clean up her mess, and she would set about sorting out beads in colour order, or become distracted with a Barbie, which she thought needed a haircut. She didn't appear to have the concentration span to clean up after herself. So often, in my fit of frustration, I would take a rubbish bin into her bedroom and clean the mess myself, only to be welcomed with another mess within the day.

Alice's pre-school teacher detected issues with her interaction with other children but couldn't put her finger on it. Her grade one teacher also detected learning and social issues, and recommended she stay down a grade. Done! Thereafter, Alice's teachers would also share their Alice frustrations with me and said she should grow out of it. Then the next year's teacher would be warned to look out for her. This went on for eight years of primary school, and four years of high school. Alice was left in both schools' *too-hard-basket*.

Ray and I lamented as she was unable to read even after two years of Grade One and one year of Grade Two.

"I'm sorry Karin, I can't help her, but I can give you a book to take home. It's called "How to Teach your Child to Read", advised her well-meaning Grade Two teacher.

Teach Alice to read! That got my blood boiling. I was having enough trouble disciplining her, teaching her to get through every day, caring for her, and putting up with her never-ending little monster antics. I was barely able to think about loving her, let alone teaching her to read!

The school was not equipped to teach her, so we drove her to a specialist reading schools after school and on Saturdays. It was soon revealed that Alice must be taught to read phonetically. The school had been teaching word recognition, and Alice, now diagnosed with Dyslexia, was unable to learn the new way. I was not surprised with her diagnosis, as her father and her brother had similar learning problems at school.

However, why had the school not helped me? We lived in a higher socio-economic suburb. In fact, many foreign wealthy families chose to live in the Rossmoyne High School Zone to give their children the best in education. This proved lucrative for my real estate sales, but not helpful for my own child's learning.

This was just the start of a long expensive campaign to find answers for Alice. As a younger child, she wore the dyslexia glasses. She was given exercises to aid her left and right brain activity. She attended extracurricular reading schools every week. She was given every opportunity to mix with children from good families. She even attended Brownies, but hated the structure, and I think the leaders hated her, too.

She was taken to doctors, school psychologists, special learning centres, and we provided for all her physical and social needs, so she would not feel out of place.

By this time, I was working closer to home, and was able to be there for her before and after school. Did things change? No! Not one bit! Alice rebelled over every decision, every assignment, every rule, and every order. She would cry and cry and cry. I can't remember one day of her life where she had not cried for hours on end. Was she just a brat? Friends and family would have a quiet word with me about tough love. However, this is where their concern, love and assistance stopped. I was screaming out for practical help, not well-meaning advice from someone who had no idea what we were dealing with.

By now, aged 17, Alice had left school, and was feeling depressed about her future. She would stay in her bedroom where she would sleep, cry, make a mess, and thump out her guitar music, usually at night while we were trying to sleep. Her only joy came from playing her guitar and doing arts and crafts. Her band mates were her only social contact. They tolerated Alice's behaviour as she was the only girl in the group, and they were fascinated with her crazy wild side. She was a real mad rock chic!

"Alice, do you think you have ADD?" I asked.

"Sure do. I've been thinking that for ages now," she replied with so much wisdom.

"Okay, let's get you checked. There must be something that can be done to help you."

Here began our second round of running about visiting psychiatrists, ADD specialists, doing questionnaires, and answering the same barrage of questioning. Why did they all live so far away from us? We were always in the car crisscrossing Perth for yet another appointment. Was there no one local who could help us?

The diagnosis of ADHD and 80% depression came with prescriptions for Dexamphetamine and anti-depressants. Right, take 6 Dexis every four hours, and 3 antidepressants every day. And that was that. No help, no assistance, no offer to teach her some life skills. Nothing. Just take your pills. Get a life, and comeback every six months to get your scripts filled again. At this point, we had a diagnosis. There was a name to her erratic poor behaviour. There were pills to help her. We were finally getting somewhere after 17 years.

Within the week, Alice had read her first book ever. Kurt Cobain's story, a famous rock star who committed suicide at the age of 27. I was proud of her for settling down to read a book and tried not to be judgemental of her reading material.

Was Alice on the verge of a fantastic, new fulfilling life? Was this the end of her crying, her anxiety, and her poor choices? Well, no! Not at all, in fact things became progressively worse.

Chapter 32

Multi-Task

"If you don't like it there, Ray, then leave," I advised, as we were going through one of his regular nightly work debriefing sessions.

"There's nothing else I can do," he bemoaned.

"Well, just leave anyway! I'll write out the resignation letter. You're just going to have to believe there is a job out there for you," I preached. With my own volatile work experiences, I had become a risk-taker with faith, and passionately believed that when one door closes, a window of opportunity would always open.

"Ray, you don't deserve to be unhappy. You've worked over and beyond the call of your duty and/or your pay packet. You've learnt so much about business and people. You're not the same unskilled, frightened man who walked into that building 18 years ago. I am so proud of how far you've come. I believe in you Ray. Resign for god's sake!"

***

The time had come for Arthur, the company owner, Ray's friend, teacher, and confidant, to sell his business and retire. The new owners, from a less successful hire business, were not giving Ray, the Transport Manager with 18 years' experience, the respect and status he believed he deserved, as a long-standing employee of that once phenomenally successful company.

New management made life increasingly difficult for Ray. It was now their way or the highway! Ray's 18 years' experience in the furniture hire business, his stalwart disposition, his strong work ethic, his amazing customer service skills, and his loyalty to the company counted for zilch. It was time to leave! However, this time, if Ray could find the courage to leave, he would not be leaving with nothing. He'd be leaving with his self-esteem intact, with relevant business skills, and his own slowly built asset base, all of which would put him in a good position to commence his own business.

After 13 years in the hire business, having learned invaluable lessons, and with good business relationships with the who's who of the hire industry throughout Perth, our son Glen left the furniture hire industry to start his own pot plant hire business. Yet, this is not Glen's story, and how his business grew from nothing to become the biggest plant hirer in Perth, only he can accurately tell. Ray and I are extremely proud of him.

"They've failed in their previous business venture, and now they're going to ruin all the great work we've spent years building. They've no idea what they're doing, and they won't listen to me. They make me so bloody angry, I feel like smashing them," he grimaced, as he expressed his rage during his nightly rants.

"You don't need to put up with them. Resign! It's that easy! Look at Glen. They pushed him to the limits, and now look at him. He's built his own successful business. If he can do it, surely you can too. Ray, you've got to believe you are a good person, and good people always win in this world," I firmly stated.

I wrote the resignation letter which Ray eventually found the courage to hand in. The burden was lifted from him, as he arrived home with the biggest smile on his face. However, that happy face soon changed to a look of fear, as he began to worry about his future. We discussed possible jobs he could do. He was convinced he was not interested in working for a boss, and not being valued or respected.

He had worked with his brothers until he was 36 years old, and that had ended with his finances, his confidence, and his self-worth in tatters. He had put the same energy into helping Arthur build his business from the early times of the America's Cup days in 1986, through to it becoming the biggest and most successful hire company in Western Australia.

Ray hinted he would really like to try working for himself but had no idea on how to go about it. He still missed the farm and would often imagine himself running his own farming business. However, that door had been well and truly slammed shut!

I set about writing a list of Ray's special skills: friendly, hard-working, loyal, loved being outdoors, self-starter, eager to please, never gives up, first to work and last to leave, no job too hard, high energy, respectful, good with machinery, takes pride in himself and his work. A list of fine qualities!

I then scanned the local newspapers, reading every advertisement, with a view to learning of the suite of services currently in demand.

My eyes were drawn to an advert from a pressure cleaning company. I recalled from my property management days that a reliable pressure cleaning company had always been among our sought-after services.

"Ray, how would you like to do pressure cleaning?" I cautiously enquired. Suddenly, as though a switch had been turned on, his sad, frightened demeanour lifted. Great excitement beamed from his face.

"Hey, where are you going?" I called out after him as he shot straight out the door.

"I'm off to do some research on it. I need to price the plant, work out transport, and learn something about the business," he yelled back. He was a man on a mission.

Within weeks, with pressure cleaning equipment purchased, a custom-made trailer, professional signage arranged, business registered, cards printed, and tax file number in place, Multitask High Pressure Cleaning was open for business.

"Now, how do I get work?" he asked, with that familiar forlorn look creeping back into his eyes. As an experienced Business Development Manager and a graduate of Public Relations, I knew the answer. I designed and printed up some flyers, handed them to him, and sent him off on his first assignment: to door knock every house in Applecross, an affluent neighbouring suburb, to enquire if he could be of assistance to them with his list of services.

That day, I became even more impressed with my husband. In my sales days, I had often tried to help new sales representatives kick-start their careers. However, whenever I had mentioned doorknocking, they would just sneer at me and say, "I wouldn't do that, even if you paid me." Well, Ray did do that, and they did pay him. His business was off and running.

Once again, using the same skills I practised in business development, we brainstormed where we could expect to source customers, which cost effective mediums we would use to advertise, how to convert each customer into a repeat client, and where to go for referral business. Having vast inside knowledge of the real estate industry, I knew the slogan "You never get a second chance to make a first impression."

I managed to sell this concept of professionally cleaning pavers and pool surrounds before selling or renting a property to salespeople and property managers alike. We also designed a speciality list of services which would see him through both the summer and winter months, as learnt when studying Service Marketing.

It was satisfying for Ray to be outdoors, away from a company environment, and able to be the creator of his own destiny. Although I worked in real estate business development by day, by night I totally enjoyed myself as I set up his Excel spreadsheets, his accounting system, and his record keeping facility. With each month came increased work. Ray's targets were being achieved as I tried to think up new ways to source more work.

"Would you please stop that?" snapped Ray, as he sat listening to me excitedly listing all the ways we could source further new business. "If you keep that up, you'll bloody-well kill me," he panicked. True, he was the sole operator. After having managed up to 40 men at his previous job, he chose not to employ anyone to work for him.

"I don't want to take anyone on, because if they are sloppy, lazy, or wreck my equipment, I couldn't cope with that. No, its best I just run my own show in my own way," he concluded.

We continued to run the business on a one-man scale, where he could give good honest service, earning respect and loyalty for his efforts. The money flowed in accordingly.

In 2008, while on a visit to check out our three investment properties, we were sitting in a restaurant overlooking the beautiful estuary in Mandurah, a picture-perfect waterside city on the south coast of Western Australia. Something within me made me say:

"Ray, how would you like to live here in Mandurah. We could enjoy these stunning sights every day." To my utter surprise, without hesitation, he replied:

"Yes, let's do it!"

"But you have your business contacts in Perth. Do you think you'll cope with the travel?"

"Driving is nothing to me. I can always make new contacts down here. You could get a real estate job in the area too. It shouldn't be half as busy or as stressful as Perth for you. If Alice doesn't want to come and live with us, she can stay in Perth. The choice will be hers, but she can't live in Bateman, we'll need to rent that house out."

So, the decision to move was made. I had already resigned from my BDM job in Canning Bridge, citing sheer exhaustion, so it didn't matter where I lived. The Rossmoyne High School zone had well and truly served its purpose, as Alice had left school years earlier. Besides, my parents had recently moved to Mandurah from Merredin, and were already living in one of our investment properties. My sister Anne and her husband were also close by.

The spacious newly built house in Lakelands, originally purchased as an investment property, was to become our new home.

It was goodbye, Perth. Hello, Mandurah!

Chapter 33

My Work Here Is Not Done

There's nothing better after a full day at a real estate seminar than to be wined and dined at the company's expense, with your six favourite colleagues, at the beautiful Busselton Abbey Beach Resort Restaurant. Not one of us had a problem in the world as we chatted, giggled, ate, drank wine, gossiped, and giggled some more.

"I don't feel like going to bed yet, it's only 8.30," chirped the lively Jennifer.

"Let's go for a walk down to the beach," she suggested.

"Okay," I and the other three females of the group, Jenny, Jill, and Moya, answered in unison.

"No, I'm not going," replied her husband Mitch, our boss and keeper of the company credit card and the unit swipe card.

"You can go, and I'll stay here and talk to Graeme." It was most apparent that by this time of the night, Graeme and Mitch were enjoying the spoils of said credit card and were hoping to settle in for another hour or so before retiring to the adjoining self-contained shared unit accommodation.

The five of us confident, free, and fifty-something-year-old ladies hurriedly left the room, laughing and giggling like tipsy teenagers on their first unsupervised night out. We kicked off our shoes and walked down the well-worn pathway towards the waterfront. What a wonderful night it was. The full moon bounced its light upon choppy waves as they washed upon the sand. Millions of twinkling stars illuminated the night sky. Leaves rustled in the light breeze. The beach was deserted, except for a few fishermen who had set up just a stone's throw from where we were standing. We paddled along bare foot in the shallow waters, as we continued to chatter about our day.

"Let's go swimming," suggested Jennifer, the alpha female among us, always a leader among her peers. She started to take off her clothes. Apprehensively, I looked around at the other ladies who appeared to be fumbling with their shirt buttons. I had never been skinny dipping in my life, not even when I had a figure worth flaunting, but there I was, on the wrong side of fifty-five, getting my gear off too. *What the heck, I do have some girlie adventures to catch up on*! Jennifer and I discarded our clothes, making a small pile on the sand, and waded out to sea, or at least to a depth that would fully cover our dignity. The other three ladies remained standing knee-deep in the water by the beach and yelled out cheeky comments like: "Sharks love to eat naked ladies as it saves them having to chew through their clothes first. White Pointers love juicy white backsides. Those fishermen can see your boobs." *Funny buggers! Jennifer and I both laughed as we were perfectly aware of our body shapes and thought the fishermen would need to have had incredible eyesight to see anything.*

Unperturbed by their warnings, we swam out to enjoy the warmth of the black moon-lit waters, no doubt resembling a pair of playful mermaids. What a wonderful experience it was to be naked in the warm sea, to be free of restrictive clothing and to be among such wonderful friends. How lucky I felt!

It soon became apparent that the other three ladies chose not to join us skinny dipping, as we could see no sign of them on the beach. *Oh well, their loss*! Jennifer and I continued to chat and frolic about naked, until we became cold and decided to head back to where we'd left our clothes. My plan was to grab my gear, race to the shadow of a tree, and get dressed quickly before I had given too much of a flash show.

Now, where did we leave our clothes? As we neared the shore, we soon discovered they were not where we'd left them. Our three lady friends were nowhere to be seen either. Had these wonderful mates, amazing colleagues, and like-minded souls taken our clothes and disappeared? *Bitches!*

Jennifer and I crept gingerly from the water, fully aware we were stark naked, fully aware there were fishermen just up the beach, but confident we were both fabulous at fifty. But we knew what to do, we were women of the world. With one hand covering our lower body, the other arm stretched across our chests, and with the word "bitches" flowing freely from our lips, we walked guardedly down the sandy tree lined track leading to our accommodation. One part of my mind hoped the men would be back at the apartment by now, to let us in, and another part of my mind hoped to God they wouldn't be.

But Mitch was the protector of the entry key card. Do we hide in the garden until they come back? Jennifer didn't mind if her husband caught her naked in the bushes, but she surely didn't want to give Graeme something to smile about for a week. And I didn't want either of them to have a picture of cold, bedraggled, naked me etched into their brain for eternity. We shivered in the moonlight as we neared our unit.

Then suddenly, from behind a huge Azalea tree, sprang three giggling middle-aged ladies with our clothes in hand. They were having the best fun ever! We grabbed our clothes, dressed quickly, and went into the unit where those once amazingly kind and thoughtful colleagues, in fits of laughter, re-lived the scene repeatedly, at Jennifer's and my expense.

The following morning, while preparing to head back to Mandurah, someone turned on the television to catch the morning news. The words: Breaking News, Breaking News, Breaking News, scrolled across the screen. The newsreader then announced: "At 9.15pm last night, a fisherman was taken by a shark, as he swam just 50 metres from the beach at Busselton's Abbey Beach Resort."

Shocked to the core, my colleagues and I glared at each other in stunned disbelief.

It seemed my work here was not done.

Chapter 34

Where There's Life, There's Hope!

"Sorry, Mummy, I don't want to live anymore," sobbed Alice, over the phone. I could hear the hopelessness in my youngest daughter's voice.

"Where are you?" I shouted.

"I'm lost in the bush somewhere. I don't want to live anymore. I don't have a place on this planet. Tim doesn't want me. I'm just a piece of shit. I've hooked up a piece of polythene pipe to the exhaust, into my car, and now I feel sleepy. Sorry, Mummy!

"Alice, get out of the car! Get out of the bloody car!" I bellowed.

"No, I don't want to." My heart felt heavy, as I sensed her scant will to live was waning. *If I could just get her to get out of the car.*

"Alice, where are you? We'll come and get you."

This was not the first time we had received a distressing phone call from her. However, they were usually cries for help. Like:

"I must have passed-out at a Melbourne nightclub, and I've just woke up in some random's house and I'm wearing someone else's clothes. I've missed my train, and there's not another one going back to Melbourne until the morning. It's so dark. I'm cold and hungry. I've been arrested. I'm so sick. I think I'm dying. A truck has just run into my car, and I think it's a write-off."

At these times, my first thoughts had always been: *where there is life, there is always hope.* Ray and I lived in hope. We hoped she'd find peace in this lifetime. We hoped she'd find love. We hoped she'd find a group of compatible friends, and we hoped she'd find happiness.

Years earlier, she'd been diagnosed with ADHD plus depression, but we, as her parents, always believed that was not her complete diagnosis. There was something else amiss, and we had made it our joint mission to give love and support, as her life played out from one depressing disaster to the next.

Alice believed she'd found love, but that relationship had deteriorated into an unhealthy, emotional dependency, and the time had come for Tim, her boyfriend of 12 months, to extricate himself from her, and to get on with his life. He'd tried so hard to be there for her, but her erratic behaviour had not improved, even when she was on her prescribed medication. The young man had finally found the courage to spell it out to her the previous night. Apparently, a physical fight, instigated by her, had ensued.

This was not the time for me to get emotional or flip out. After having this precious yet challenging little girl in my life for the past 29 years, I knew full well, if I became hysterical, she would just hang up the phone. By now, I knew the drill.

"Alice, look out of the window. What do you see?"

"It's just bush. Umm, there are some tall chimneys."

"Okay, can you hear anything?"

"No, but I did hear a train a little while ago."

"Was it an electric train or a diesel train?"

"I don't know, it was a noisy long one."

"Did you recognise any of the streets on your way there?"

"No, it was dark, and I was crying too much, but I think it's a road Dad sometimes uses to come home." She hung up.

I kept telling myself *don't lose it, don't lose it,* as I dialled triple zero.

"What is your emergency?" asked the professional sounding voice at the other end of the phone.

"Umm, I don't really know. My daughter has just called to say she's in the bush somewhere, and has hooked the exhaust pipe into her car, and has told me she wanted to die," I stumbled.

"Do you know the location?"

"From the questions I asked, I think she may be near the Kwinana factories, in the bush, quite near the railway line." I went on to give her Alice's mobile number with the hope it could be cyber tracked. I also gave the make, registration, and colour of her car. They asked my contact details, which I readily gave.

"Stay there," she commanded, "I'll put the call out now."

I abruptly hung up and called out to Ray, "I'll be dammed if I'm sitting around while our little girl is out there. Come on, let's go and find her!"

We raced out to Ray's car, and headed off from Lakelands, north towards Kwinana, some 30 kilometres away.

As we drove, I dialled Alice's phone number. My heart was pounding so fast. I was in a state of quiet panic. Relief washed over me when she answered.

"Mummy, I'm scared. I can't breathe very well. It stinks in here. Why is it taking so long? I don't want to be here. I'm a piece of shit."

"Alice, get out of the car. Just get out of the fucking car!" I frantically screamed down the phone. "Just get out. Open a door, open a window. Whatever you've done, whatever, I don't care, just get out of the bloody car." She hung up.

"Ray, drive faster." I shrieked. "We don't have much time! Alice needs us. We can't let her down!" My heart was in my stomach, or was my stomach in my heart? My emotions became numb. My head was clouded with panic and terror. My breathing became short as I abused Ray for driving within the speed limit. Ray drove calmly. I couldn't detect which emotion he was experiencing. However, this was not the time to discuss feelings. This was the time to move our backsides and find our lost daughter before it was too late. My phone rang. I recognised the number as my neighbour Donna.

"What's happening?" she asked. "I've got the police here. They're at your house. I saw you and Ray shoot off earlier, so I came over to see if I could help them."

"Tell them we couldn't sit around while our Alice is lost in the bush and possibly dying. Get them to tell you all about it. Sorry, Donna, but get off the phone. I need it in case she calls me." I phoned Alice again with the hope she'd pick up. She did.

"Alice, we are not far away. Can you give me an idea where you are? Anything! Just anything. Can you get out of the car and walk towards the road where we can see you?"

"Trucks fill up here," she quietly sobbed. *Okay, Karin, think!* I ordered myself. *Rockingham Road, trucks fill up, tall chimneys, trains.*

"Ray, she's up there opposite the Speedway. Hurry, for God's sake," I screamed. As we approached the area where I suspected she may be, we saw a curled-up body lying just off the side of the road. I recognised the clothing as those Alice had worn the evening before. Abruptly, Ray stopped the car alongside her as I scrambled out.

"I'm sorry, mummy, I'm sorry. I'm sorry!" she cried.

"My darling, it's okay, it's okay. We're here." I said in a contrived soothing voice. I threw myself down on the gravel to lie with her and wrapped my arms tightly around her long bony body. A sense of relief flooded through me as we lay together on the ground, both sobbing uncontrollably. Ray headed off down a sandy bush track near the railway line to find her car. I glanced up to the sky and saw a white, fixed wing aircraft overhead. My mobile phone rang.

"This is the constable, from the WA Police, is that you down there?"

"We've found her, we've got her," I cried. "Her father searching for her car now. She got out of the car. I'm sorry, I couldn't sit at home waiting. I had to find her!"

"Take her to Rockingham Hospital. They are waiting and will admit her immediately," he instructed.

"Thank you, thank you, I'll take her there now." Alice lay semi-conscious in the foetal position on the front seat of her car, as I drove the ten kilometres to the hospital. Nothing was said. On arrival, we were immediately ushered through emergency, where she was fitted with an oxygen mask and hospitalised for several days.

Thank God she's alive. Where there's life, there is always hope! But, what now?

***

This was not her first nor her last cry for help. Each self-inflicted threat to her life had been strategically planned, but, thankfully, not well executed.

After a series of failed attempts, the lead psychiatrist at the local hospital finally took notice of her frailty and found her a six-month placement in an Art Therapy Group. There she thrived. She loved the arts and crafts sessions, and her relationships with the psychologists. However, she showed no interest or emotion towards the other day-patients. She did not ask their names, nor did she have any rapport with them.

At the completion of the program, I said, "Alice, instead of thinking about how to die, I suggest you start thinking about how you'd like to live."

"Yes, I've been thinking the same thing. I think I'll travel. I've always wanted to go to France, and snowboard in the French Alps." So, with much research, her meagre savings and mostly our savings, she managed to be accepted on a "work-away" experience of a lifetime in France the following year.

However, Alice did not realise she would be taking her problems with her. Neither did I realise that I would be living each of those days vicariously, as I guided her via Facetime, Facebook, and Messenger, through the highs and lows of her emotions. It was now my responsibility to liaise with her psychiatrist in relation to her prescriptions, and to send "Schedule 1" drugs to oversees destinations. Each month I'd send her a care package containing her 30-day allocation of Dexamphetamine, antidepressants, Pawpaw Ointment (for her frozen cracked lips) and, of course, I included several tubes of Vegemite for my Aussie abroad.

Chapter 35

The Love Of A Dog

I think I'll get a dog! How else does one force oneself to walk around the block every morning and night. It's not like I'm a fitness enthusiast.

My sudden determination that I must have a dog in my life was for a perfectly selfish reason. I needed one to drag me kicking and screaming around the block twice a day, to reduce the size of my derriere. I was never known as a pet lover. Just ask my friends of old. I'd totally ignored their pets in the hope they'd stay away from me. I never ever wanted a bunny or a kitten. I certainly never wanted a parrot that talked. I didn't want a bowl of little fish, because as the 1950s song (Pattie Page - How Much is That Doggy in the Window) goes: you can't take a goldfish for walks.[7]

Fitness self-motivation was never my forte, so I needed something to inspire me to go outdoors and walk my butt off. A dog was my only solution! I'd never had my own pet before. Ray's belief in relation to owning a dog was that they must earn their keep, a sentiment from his farming past. Since we were now living in suburbia, he reminded me that they did poo everywhere.

Yes, I did have a vague disgusting memory of my real estate days when I once got poop on my stilettos during a house inspection. My husband's final argument was "You can't shut the bastards up." A recollection of a past neighbour's Red Setter. Yes, I'd been listening to these objections for most of my life, however, something in my spirit was telling me I truly needed to get a little white dog.

In secret, I proceeded to make phone calls to local pet stores, to no avail. I asked my puppy-loving colleagues, "Where can I buy a dog?" They refused to tell me. I suspected they feared I'd be an unworthy pet owner. I drove to K9 Rescue, just out of Mandurah, hoping to find a stray for minimal cost. Free would have been more my desired price bracket. However, those poor little imprisoned orphans didn't fit the picture I'd

---

[7] Merrill, Bob, *"(How Much Is) That Doggie in The Window?"* sung by Pattie Page, Mercury Records, USA. 1952

formed of myself: active wear, tight tushy, cute puppy, matching outfits. *No, they're all too big, and far too scruffy for my requirements.*

I'd been warned that puppies do lots of poos anywhere and everywhere, and I'd be responsible to pick up the poo-poo in one of those little yellow bags and carry it home. I must admit, the thought repulsed me! Dogs, they say, need constant attention, some even want to sleep in your bed. *Ha ha, I could imagine Ray's reaction to that idea!* I may concede to let a dog sleep in the laundry, but the thought of it running around the house and sleeping on the bed? Well, that would be downright unhygienic! Well-meaning friends explained that dogs are expensive to feed, and the cost of vet care could be horrendous. It was also pointed out that once you get a pet, you're stuck with it until it dies. *Wow. Sounds permanent!* Such practical advice and issues had never crossed my mind. My thoughts were wholly and solely on the tight, muscular backside.

At this point I hadn't even considered the initial cost of the animal. *Shouldn't be too much! May even be free!* It would be easier to present the idea to Ray as a *fait accompli* if it were free.

I searched the internet to find a puppy for sale. And there she was! An eight-week-old white Maltese Shih Tzu Cross. *What a sweetheart! Well, I know I'm not going to get Ray's support, so I'll drive the 75 kilometres to the Mount Lawley Puppy Shop after work to meet her anyway.*

Alice was my one and only ally. On entering the store, we could hear dogs barking, yapping, and squealing. For *God's sake, shut-up*! I asked to be shown the little white cutie in the blue fluffy jacket, as featured on the internet. The staff member handed me a clean white shirt to place over my clothes, apparently so I didn't contaminate the animal. They handed me the little white puppy. I held her close, as she snuggled up on to my shoulder and placed her tiny nose under my chin. I bent my head to feel her warmth on my neck. Our eyes meet. She licked my cheek.

Suddenly, the heavens opened. *Is it my imagination or do I really hear a chorus of angels singing love songs from on high*? My heart expanded, as the magic of love entered my being. Enchantment surrounded as we clung tight to each other. We were falling in love. I knew my life would never be the same again. If necessary, it would be my doggie, and me against the world. I vowed to love and protect her. I made a pact: I'll put a magic spell on Ray, and he will love her too. I promised she would not have to walk around the block until she felt strong enough to do so. I then knew there was nothing in this world I now would not do for her.

"I love you," I whispered into her tiny fluffy floppy ear. I then made a quick flit around the store to gather up the must-have accessories for pet ownership.

"I'll take the puppy and these," I said to the shop attendant.

"That will be $1,600 for the dog and $198 for the leash, the food, the shampoo, the jacket, the collar, and the picture from out of the window," she replied.

Oops, I realised I had forgotten to ask a vital question: *how much is that doggy in the window?* I tried not to blaspheme, to appear shocked or even to drop the puppy, as I reached for my Mastercard. *Gees, how am I going to explain this one to Ray?* I proceeded to make the long drive home to Mandurah singing doggie love songs, like '*Love, Love me Do* '[8] and '*You Ain't Nothing but a Hound Dog.* '.[9]

It was a winter's evening as Alice, and I excitedly walked through the door carrying our precious purchase. There was no food cooking on the stove, and the house was freezing cold. Ray had been worried about me when he'd arrived home to find the house in darkness. To my surprise, he glanced at the little white puppy wrapped in its polka-dot blanket, and his heart obviously melted, just like mine had done only an hour before. He reached for the puppy in my arms. The only question asked was,

"Is it a girl?"

"Yes," I replied, wondering when he was going to ask me the real nitty gritty questions such as, "How much was it and why didn't we discuss this first?"

"Good, let's call her Poppy." He'd always remembered the hair oil he used as a boy, "Californian Poppy," and just loved saying it. It had become his pet-name when referring to his granddaughters, and anything else that resembled cute.

---

[8] Lennon, John and Paul McCartney. *"Love Me Do,"* The Beatles, Parlophone, UK. 1962
[9] Lieber, Jerry and Mike Stoller, *"Hound Dog,"* Originally released by Big Mama Thornton, USA. 1952

To cut a long love story short, that night, Poppy, scared of her new surroundings, slept in the safety of our bed, cuddled in my arms. A place of comfort she still seeks on a nightly basis. Ray fell in love with her immediately and didn't ask how much I paid for her. Years later, I broached the subject, "Why haven't you ever asked how much I paid for Poppy?"

"The cost isn't important. I love that little girl too." *It couldn't have been too much*, or so he thought.

But how do you care for a puppy when you work full time? That was easy. Within a year, thanks to Ray's business success, I was able to give up working after 33 years in the real estate industry and could then spend my day ensuring my puppy had all the love, exercise and treats she desired. It was also good therapy for Alice to have a dog in the house. Something else for her to love, along with Misty, her black cat.

To this day, my old friends are still coming to terms with my unashamed pet loving nature. They still have horrific memories of me being the animal hater, the hard-faced woman of old, and are amused with my 180-degree change in persona.

Poppy and I walk twice daily and, as far as her toilet habits are concerned, I lovingly rush to pick up her poo-poo with one of those little yellow bags. No big deal! Oh, and my derriere doesn't appear to be any smaller. Darn! But Poppy is looking hot!

The love I instantly felt for Poppy inspired me to write my first poem ever, so excuse me while I indulge myself.

Poppy

The first time I heard your whimper and I turned around
My heart went kaboom, truly it was love at first sight
Your beautiful mournful eyes begged me to take you home
I didn't know then how much you'd set my soul alight

Out of my comfort zone, shopping for your clothes not mine
Polka dot raincoat, matching leash, and many bling collars
The way you turn heads each day, with your fashion so chic
Just don't disclose the price I paid, so many dollars

We're chilled out in this household, we've all become mellow
Forgiveness, tolerance, joyful emotions run high
No more raised voices, just love-talk and happy laughter
We love you so much, we never want to say goodbye

With Maxi Cat and sister Alice, you love to hang
Catching ball, playing toys, even a swim at the beach
Happy to see other doggies pass, you run so fast
and run so far, but those seagulls are never in reach

My heart couldn't love you more, I know you feel the same
It's in your adoring eyes, in your warmth, your greeting
I say your name, smile, you're impossible to ignore
Thank you for love, I came alive at our first meeting

Chapter 36

The Times, They Are A Changing

"How old are you? asked the Perth-based franchise owner of the Mandurah office I'd poured my heart and soul into for the past five years.

"Fifty-nine" I replied. I wanted to add, "would you believe?" thinking he was going to compliment me on my youthful looks.

"Have you ever thought of retiring?" he replied. *What? My ego just taken an almighty blow. The cheeky so-and-so! Why would I retire when I was doing my dream job with my dream colleagues?*

On my arrival in Mandurah, I'd answered an advert, "We're Searching for a Super-Star" and at the time, truly believed I fitted that description perfectly. After several rounds of interviews, I got the job, and was employed for the newly created position of Business Development Manager. Once again, no one in this high-profile franchised office had any idea on what a BDM did, but management conceded they needed one.

They wanted to grow their rent roll organically, as opposed to buying another agent's rent roll. Once again, I was shown a desk and was ordered *to get stuck into it*. There was no corporate blueprint, no guidance, and no input from anyone from the office hierarchy. Well, that was fine with me, as, once again, I utilised the same skills as per my previous ten years BDM experience.

Being a highly visual person, I created a colour coded Excel spreadsheet to track my daily contacts and activity. This was my own design, which ensured I kept regular contact with every person I'd ever dealt with in the name of that company. I totally owned that job!

I found I was soon achieving my targets, and with each successful month, somehow, these targets were raised for me by management at their meetings. That was no problem, I could do whatever was expected of me, even though it was draining my energy and time, seven days a week.

As the years rolled by, things started to change. New computer inter-office programs were being introduced. I was asked to enter all my contacts onto a corporate data base and then, it seemed, someone higher up the marketing food chain in Sydney would email my clients corporate news, advertising material and opportunities to win competitions. As I had always taken an old fashion personal approach to dealing with my people, I was horrified. In my eyes, these were my contacts. I cared about them as real live people. I had walked through their homes, had drunk their coffee, laid my knowledge before them, and listened to their plans and dreams for their future. I had won their hearts, as I listed their property for management with my company. To me, these were real people, and now they were to become prospects on a corporate data base.

The sales reps and I were encouraged to set up our own Facebook business page, have a Linked-in account, and to use Twitter and even Instagram to convey our daily messages to the public. Some of the younger tech-savvy reps set up their own YouTube accounts and were videoing their own promotional material. We were introduced to iPads and were expected to be able to zip around the screen from program to program, as we pointed out local listings and sales statistics to our prospective customers. It seemed a 30-minute iPad lesson at the Apple head office was supposed to have made me sufficiently proficient to have mastered the entire suite of real estate programs ever invented. No further training or assistance was ever offered to me by management.

In my day, an agent put in hours and hours of learning the local market and was able to expound their knowledge while looking a client straight in the eye. But no, we can't do that anymore! Now, we were to bore the butt off clients by zooming about a screen, illustrating our computer prowess, as we referred to dubious (often inaccurate) data, rather than winning their business and respect with our own market knowledge and expertise.

I had loved working at that office. I'd built a good working relationship with each member of staff. I knew them as friends first and colleagues second. Once again, we all worked hard, but didn't we know how to celebrate? Never had I the confidence or the opportunity to dress up in fancy costumes, but here at party central I was in my element, as a burlesque dancer, a beauty queen, a bridesmaid, a mutton dressed-up as lamb, a bogan bride, and a golden girl in a big gold fifties style dress. We holidayed in Bali together, walked marathons, attended dances, celebrated birthdays in style, and even participated in the town's Christmas Street parades.

Until that moment, when asked about my impending retirement plans, I hadn't even contemplated ever leaving that safe happy place. I had never once thought about my apparent impending use-by date. So, what was the owner trying to say to me? I was shocked he had even hinted at my retirement. He was at least 5 years older than me. Surely, I must have appeared full of youth and vitality in comparison. He was still working. However, eventually, I wasn't surprised when I learnt of his ulterior motive: get the old girl out and swing the young pretty tech savvy one in.

After consideration, I decided it would be perfect timing to bow out gracefully while still on a high. I suppose there is only so much of "well, in my day, before mobile phones and computers were invented, we used to … blah, blah blah …" my colleagues could put up with. I knew the times were changing, and if I could not, or would not, keep up with the new modes of marketing, my old era mindset may well have caused me future embarrassment.

I decided to leave it to the young ones. Let them worry about the owner's rent roll. Let them work overtime. Let them mop up the aftermath of the boom times, and let them become robots, as they follow the step-by-step instructions on their latest computer programs and data bases. Real estate was becoming barely recognisable. It had become all about data bases, algorithms, and apps. Public relations, my speciality, was now outmoded. So old school!

I did go on to work as a BDM further up the coast north of Mandurah for a small family real estate company. However, I found my heart just wasn't in it, nor was the property managers heart, nor the owner's. All of which spelt disaster! The property manager turnover was of a revolving door nature, the owner's mental health declined for the very worst, and I was left wondering why I was putting so much energy into a sinking ship. Within a year, I asked for reduced hours which eventually dwindled to one day a week.

I finally worked it out: I did not want to work for money. In my mind I had never worked a day in my life. The jobs I had done were not work, they were lifestyle choices, a privilege to serve, an innate skill I had to share with people. However, in true universe form, the money always flowed in. In my first week of real estate, some 33 years before, a wise man told me: "If you help enough people get what they want, you in turn will get everything you want."

Now, working just one day a week. I realised I was only there for the money. I did not even like the job, as I sat there subservient to my boss's instructions. I dreaded that day.

Besides, I had a puppy at home I really wanted to be with. *It was time to say goodbye.*

What a relief it was to have finally found total freedom. What a luxury it was to not feel guilty, to be able to sit at home in my cane egg chair cuddling Poppy, amongst my much-loved plants, to be makeup free, wearing active wear whilst being totally inactive if I so chose. I finally had choice. I had the time to concentrate on Alice's needs, the choice to walk my dog, and the luxury to unearth my own suppressed passions.

My thirty-three-year sentence in my self-imposed *real estate prison* was over. Real estate, where my financial goals had been achieved, and the world had become my oyster.

Chapter 37

Auf Wiedersehen Anna

"Mum has just died," my sister Anne cried over the phone.

I stood in stunned disbelief. Die? My mother wouldn't die, even though she had been threatening to for as long as I could remember. I knew she'd been in poor health over the past ten years, but die?

Our dear mother had finally succumbed to organ failure, her heart had just had enough. Every organ in her tired frame had given her cause for concern over the years, and now her poor body just fell to the ground and gave up on her.

Anna Philapina Lorek, nee Schwarz entered the world on 14th December 1931. Her spirit left us on 7th April 2014. That is exactly 82 years 3 months and 23 days of living, loving, giving, working, supporting, learning, and yearning. A full life which I will condense into mere paragraphs. It hardly gives a life justice!

At her funeral, I was privileged to speak about my mother, and told of the many roles she had played to perfection during her long and fruitful life. As a wife, Anna followed her beloved husband to the end of the earth and supported him in all he'd ever wanted to do. This is a story of a woman standing by her man through thick and thin, and, together, conquering their life's challenges.

As a mother, she led by example, and prepared her three daughters well for marriage. Each of us were graduates of the "Anna Lorek Academy of Housewifery," majoring in cooking, cleaning, ironing, sewing, embroidery, and doing each of these chores whilst singing in German. With commando-like discipline, she drilled into her girls the traits of an excellent work ethic, resilience, and tenacity. Today my sisters and I agree that these qualities have served us well during our own lives, even though we have often been accused of taking them to the extreme. Too well trained!

As a woman of Lutheran faith, Anna raised her girls with Christian values, which prepared us for own roads ahead. The church became our social conscience, our weekly meeting place for locals of German extraction, a replacement of our missing family, and gave each of us an opportunity to shine and/or gain social standing within our small community.

As a Mother-in-law, Anna had three devoted sons-in-law whom she loved beyond reproach. In her eyes Alvan, Michael, and Ray could do no wrong, so it must have been their wives' fault if there was ever an argument.

"Don't come running home to me if you split up, but I will take in each of your husbands if you do," she would say. Consequently, with nowhere to go, no sympathy forthcoming, and carrying all blame after any argument, my sisters and I would always stay home and sort out our own marital problems, without involving Mum in any way.

As the Proprietors of the Merredin Standard Laundry, Anna and Harald built a solid business with a sound reputation for service and integrity. Yes, they worked hard. As a family, we all contributed to the running of the business. We knew that without the business, our parents would not have had the finances, the social standing in the town, or the respect that the locals were finally paying to *New Australians*. The family had come a long way since first landing in the Merredin Shire, on the back of an old utility, all those years ago.

As a Lions Lady, Anna worked continually behind the scenes to support Lion Harald in all his community endeavours and leadership aspirations. Dad was the social butterfly, the funny one, the personality personified, and Mum would stand in his shadow, quite often shaking her head, as he endeared himself to the entire community. My parents travelled Australia and the world as representatives of Lions International.

As a church steward, Anna organised, cleaned, cooked, worked at the church op shop, and did anything she could to assist in the smooth running of her local parish. These years were a happy time for Mum, as she became depended upon by the church members for her organisational skills. She loved to feel needed and thrived in this role.

As a friend, Anna freely welcomed people into her home. Her love of cooking, her Black Forrest Tortes, and her hospitality will long be remembered by all who had the privilege to be invited into her home. Mum was house proud, and I recall Saturday mornings when we would scrub down the entire inside of the house to within an inch of its life. I was led to believe this was a normal practice, but in later life was surprised to find that most people don't scrub everything as often, if not, at all. Shock horror for me when I discovered that!

As a grandmother, Anna owned the rights to utterly spoil each of her seven grandchildren: Darren, Glen, Justin, Erica, Nathaniel, Jason, and Alice. By this time of life, Mum had mellowed, and insisted on cooking the grandchildren's favourite high sugar, high fat meals, allowed them to mess her house up, and even permitted them to talk at the table. Those days, every word that came out of their mouths was deemed to be cute, clever, even interesting. *Well, that didn't happen in my day!*

As a great grandmother to eighteen, Anna delighted in the fruits of her life, as each new-born was presented to her. I'm sure she would have wondered how just three daughters could produce so many great grand-children, but she was honoured and proud to meet them all. Having arrived in Australia with two and a half children and just two suitcases, Mum and Dad would often marvel at how large the family had grown, and how truly blessed they were.

As a sibling, Anna is remembered by her brothers and sisters as the big sister they hardly knew, who followed her man to Australia to seek a new life. Being an avid writer, Mum would write letters to her brothers and sisters, send photos of her Australian family, and tell them about this land of opportunity. Not one sibling chose to join her, although four of them did eventually come for a visit in their later years.

Anna was often homesick for German family and homeland. On these occasions, Dad, who no longer had a desire to ever return to Germany, would send her back for a holiday. Her last trip was less than a year before she died, when she insisted on going home unaccompanied to say *auf wiedersehen* to her surviving family. By now, Dad's heart was no longer in Germany, but down at the Dawesville Cut, where he would take every opportunity to go fishing with his mates.

As a woman, Anna had a great love for her home and family, but even until her passing, a huge part of her heart had always remained in Ingelheim am Rhein.

After her death, Ray and I returned Mum's ashes to her hometown, where we scattered them in the shallow waters by the banks of the river Rhein, the exact spot where she, her siblings, and cousins had played as children.

In my heart, I believe she was happy to be back home at last.

Chapter 38

Opportunities Keep Knocking

"Would you write the eulogy for my sister's funeral?" asked my dear friend, in her time of grief.

"I'd be honoured. I'll write it, and you can read it."

"Nooo, I hate speaking in front of a crowd, I'll break down. Could you read it for me?"

Noting her fear of public speaking, I agreed.

Humbled yet exhilarated by the success of that experience, I decided to study *Funeral Celebrancy* through the Academy of Celebrancy, a nationally recognised training facility. My plan was to become competent to assist bereaved families in their time of need. Once again, in study mode, I attended the lectures, participated in class, and spent the next two months completing the required assignments. I was in my element, as I enjoyed writing, research, and completing my presentations.

At the completion of that course, it was recommended I also complete the *Marriage Celebrancy* course. Having enjoyed the previous one, I was excited to be back in the classroom. Once again in study mode, I was required to plan weddings, write vows, read the Marriage Act 1961, design procedures, study the legalities of each document, learn to counsel engaged couples, and study the Code of Conduct for Celebrants.

This course proved to be more extensive and demanding than the previous one as, there were lawful factors to cover. Unlike other documentation I'd worked with, marriage documents needed to be completed correctly the first time, and there was no second chance to get it right. To stuff up a marriage document would mean the couple were not legally married. Litigation could follow.

With my *Certificate IV in Celebrancy,* and three new references from notaries in hand, I set about preparing the documentation for my application to the Commonwealth governing body to apply for a Marriage Celebrant's Licence.

I cast my mind back to my real estate days when, just occasionally, there would be a hiccough with a property contract. The buyers and/or the purchasers had so often displayed the worst side of their personality, and always looked for someone to blame. *My goodness, this could be worse*. The thought of witnessing a loving fiancée turn from princess to bridezilla in 60 seconds was more than I was prepared to put myself up for.

I thought back to the placid, consenting, yet unhappy bride, I had been. There were no arguments or expensive fancy ideas from me. Not in my day. However, the brides of today appeared to be competitive. They knew exactly what they wanted: the dream of being a princess for a day seemed foremost on their minds, and woe betide anyone who ruined their day. Getting married "for better or for worse, until death do us part," appeared to be the last thing on their mind.

Recalling how difficult I had found married life, how hard we had worked to remain married, with divorce not being an option, I suddenly believed I had no right to put others through it. As much as I grew to love and respect my husband as a wonderful man, early on in my married life I discovered that the institution was not a bed of roses. In my spirit, I felt I could not be a party to the stress, the false pomp, the expensive ceremony, love turning into hate, and the shattered dreams I had witnessed with so many of my family and friends.

To me, marriage is between two people. A legal obligation, not a competition, a status symbol, or a destination. The signed nuptial form is recorded with the Births, Deaths, and Marriages Department to keep track of who's with who in Australia. In earlier times, birth and death registrations were kept in churches, the principal governing body of the day.

Hence, the churches were involved with recording the marriage agreement, and the registrations of birth through child baptism. With all due respect for the institution of marriage, both parties don't even have to love each other. The law states they must have entered the union willingly, without being coerced, and in accordance with the laws of this country. They must be over 18, unless there has been a special dispensation given by the courts, and a registration fee must be paid. No registration fee, no marriage!

I also learnt it is just as easy to get married as it is to get divorced, providing it is carried out lawfully, and registered with the appropriate governing bodies, and a fee is paid. Talk about taking the starry-eyed romance out of it. Today, the words marriage and divorce are often found in the same sentence. *Oh, my goodness, my intolerance of fake values is surfacing!*

At that time, I also disagreed with the *Marriage Act 1961*, which clearly stated: *according to Australian law, marriage is between a man and a woman.* In my lifetime I had witnessed just as much love and dedication between same sex couples, and it upset me that the law discriminated against them.

Therefore, I decided to concentrate on renewal of marriage vows, and being a funeral celebrant instead. With every funeral I was asked to lead, I felt it an absolute honour to be a part of the life celebration for their dearly departed. To be sitting with the bereaved family prior to the funeral, taking notes, learning about the life of their loved one, writing the eulogy, and then performing the celebrant's duties, has been one of the most rewarding tasks I have ever had the privilege to be involved in.

However, I soon learnt that regular work as a funeral celebrant was a closed shop. I personally visited every funeral director within a twenty-kilometre radius of my home, and found they used a member of their own staff, or a celebrant from their own stable. Although I have received assignments through friends and local funeral homes, I found the work to be sporadic, and usually with truly short notice, probably because their regular person had fallen ill, or was too busy.

If I wanted regular work, I was going to have to resort to advertising and self-promotion to get my name out there. Just like real estate, it would be back to Facebook, websites, Instagram, and the whole suite of technology I'd tried so hard to avoid. Yes, algorithms, Apps, and data bases. *What did this teach me? Get with the program old girl or get out!*

Fortunately, I don't need to work as a funeral celebrant to realise any financial ambitions and am just honoured to be of service to families in need when that special time arises.

Chapter 39

Mad Max

"I wish someone would drop a kitty-cat on my doorstep," wrote Alice on her Facebook page. "That way, I wouldn't need to choose out of all the cute cats in the world. They're all so beautiful. I'd want all of them!" Alice's dreams had always tugged at my heart's strings, as there were few events, things or people that motivated her to want anything. Her previous cat Misty, inherited from a flatmate, had died the previous year, and left a huge hole in her already sensitive heart.

The following day, while I was at the local vet for Poppy's yearly immunisation, I casually asked. "Do you know of a cat that needs to be re-homed?"

"Well, a cat has just been brought in a minute ago. Would you like to see it?" I recalled seeing a small white cat in an old wire bird cage, carried in by a lady while we waited in reception, and thought it was a strange crate for a cat, but understood not everyone had the luxury of being able to afford the latest in pet carriers.

"I'd love to." My answer may well have sounded over the top excited, because excited I was. This cat could solve a whole heap of problems for me as far as keeping my housebound daughter happy. I loved giving her surprises, even if most of them were neither wanted nor appreciated! I made myself comfortable in a chair in reception, as I eagerly awaited the introduction to our prospective new family member. The vet appeared from the next room holding the rusty wire cage in which crouched a small pure white, short haired cat. She removed the little cutie out of the carrier and handed it to me for our first cuddle.

As quick as the perfect little creature hit my lap, it arched its back, showed its hackles, let out an unholy high pitched, eardrum shattering MEOW, brought out his claws, and proceeded to scratch the living daylights out of me. Blood streamed from my face, from my arms, my hands, and my torso region, as its sharp claws ripped and punctured my skin. The shocked vet attempted to detach the animal from my body, but with every tug from her, the little bugger dug its claws in even deeper.

Its meows became louder, blood curdling. Anyone would have thought that it was me stabbing him, not the opposite.

Eventually, the vet managed to unhook the cat, and quickly put it back in the cage. A nurse appeared on the scene with sterile swabs and began to mop up the streams of blood from my body, as she tried to stem the flow. My fresh, bright red B negative blood had splattered on everything and anyone within a metre radius of where I was sitting, on my white dog, the floor, the walls, the chairs, my handbag and, of course, my clothes. You may say I was dressed in CATastrophe!

The vet staff had horrified looks on their faces, as I'm sure they feared I would demand compensation, or they may need to euthanize the wild beast. In a state of shock, or was it delirium? I said: "Okay, I'll take him." I didn't want them to think I couldn't handle a little discomfort. My pride was at stake here. Besides, I've never been one to give up on a challenge that easily. The poor little soul was frightened, or perhaps wasn't used to dogs, and Poppy was sitting on the chair close to me.

"Um, oh, um er." She sounded surprised. "That will be two hundred dollars, but first he'll have to be desexed and microchipped."

So began our adventures with Max. Alice's face lit up when I told her we could pick up the little cutie the following morning, but we'd have to be gentle with him, as he was to be sterilised that evening. The next day, armed with a modern plastic pet carrier, we eagerly drove to collect our newest family member.

"Wow, he's a screamer," announced the vet as she stuffed the cat, wearing a small Elizabethan collar, into our carrier. I had no idea what she meant, and assumed he was just upset about losing his manhood.

"Okay, little man. No rusty old bird cage for you anymore," I promised. This little guy was going to be much loved, and would be made welcome, doted on, and loved, just like Poppy. On arriving home, the cat was let out of its cage, and immediately proceeded to pace the perimeters of the inside of our house, his alertness resembling a hunter on patrol.

"He'll settle down," promised Alice. "They do this to check out their territory." By evening, Alice was still trying to befriend the little fellow, but it repeatedly rejected her advances, and kept extricating itself from her grasp. Suddenly, it let out an almighty yowl, so ear piercing and reminiscent of his screams at the vet's surgery the previous day.

"Wow, that was loud," I commented, being the biggest understatement of my lifetime. I wanted so much for Alice and the cat to form a bond. She needed all the love she could get, even if it she could only accept it from an animal. That entire night, the cat, which we named Max, continued to prowl the house, letting out the loudest screams imaginable. *Oh my God. What the heck did I just buy?* I so much wanted a cute little kitty to sooth Alice's often frazzled nerves. This cat was not fitting that criteria.

No sleep was had by any members of the household that night. And not the next and not the next. We tried to placate it. We tried to feed it. We tried to cuddle it. Joke! We bought it toys with wobbly bits, to no avail. I'd never heard such loud blood-curdling screams coming from an animal so small. In fact, I'd never heard that noise coming from a large animal either.

After several days of this performance, Alice decided to google *noisy white cats.* This is when we discovered that we had paid good money for a Deaf White Cat. It seems many pure white cats have a genetic trait which not only gives them blue eyes but also causes deafness. On reading the Facebook page, we saw lots and lots of Maxes. From the photos posted, all the cats resembled each other, and each owner had a story of woe about their DWC's loud screams, how the cats didn't like to be cuddled or tamed, and their finicky habits.

Consequently, we joined the Deaf White Cat Society of the world. Alice spoke, via the internet, to owners from English speaking countries who related similar experiences. She had found a kindred sister and brotherhood.

But what do we do? The noise was not only loud, but it was also constant, and just so annoying! What could we do? We couldn't take him back to the vet. We feared he may end up as cray-bait if anyone else adopted him, so we set about learning to love him unconditionally.

As with all my previous life challenges, my only solutions had ever been unconditional love. Now, this was just another test!

We discovered he loved to be outdoors and may well have been feral before being delivered to the vet's doorstep. However, once outdoors, he would disappear over the fence immediately, and we'd spend the next few hours walking the streets searching for him. We called him our little escapologist and joked that he must be a Russian cat. Names ranging from *Nickoffski, Pissoffski to F*#kovski* were bandied about, as by day we walked the streets, door knocking and checking every imaginable hiding place. By night Ray, Alice, and I armed ourselves with torches, and systematically shone our lights under cars, into gardens and on roof tops.

Here began the adventures of "Mad Max." The mischief he managed to get himself into will, I'm sure, be worthy of a kid's book. That will be my next venture. The illustrations will be hilarious!

One particularly noteworthy inclusion will be the day Ray went to work in his utility, pulling his Multitask trailer. First stop for the day was to have a haircut. After twenty minutes, he made his way down to the estuary foreshore, where he checked in on one of his jobs, before driving several more kilometres to a real estate office. As Ray was talking to an office lady in the car park, the staff member exclaimed:

"Hey, a white cat has just jumped off your trailer!"

Ray turned around to see Maxi cat sitting in the car park. The cat had been sleeping on top of Ray's trailer that morning. Max must have stayed asleep while Ray was at the barber, on the town tour, and only woke up once his ride had stopped. Our minds boggled, as we thought of what could have happened if the cat had awoken while Ray was at the shopping centre, or even while he was driving.

That was not the only time that happened. There was a second time when Ray forgot to check the top of his trailer before heading off to work. On reaching his destination some 20 kilometres away, Ray went to open the rear door of his trailer, glanced up, and saw Maxi peering over the edge of the trailer roof.

And so, the escapades with Maxi Cat began, as the cute white feline used the super six fences, his suburban highway, to venture into neighbourhood backyards. Facebook shame posts began to appear on the Lakelands Page, of him eyeing off neighbours' chooks, fighting with dogs, leading innocent cats astray, and scratching a kid who wanted to cuddle him. Once, he was discovered sleeping on a neighbour's pile of white toilet rolls in their house.

The cleaner almost died of fright when the toilet rolls started to move. Maxi was even found crouching in a neighbour's birdcage just watching their birds. Some of the stories are funny, some are blood thirsty, some involve his escapologist tendencies, and our efforts to

Max-proof our house and yard. For example: the day Alice took a chain-saw to my much-loved garden trees.

"What are you doing? It's taken me years to grow them," I screamed.

"Max climbs them, then clambers over the roof of our house, and goes off on one of his journeys," explained Alice, feeling totally justified in destroying my garden.

Some stories are mysteries, some are only plain ridiculous, but not one story is about a cute cuddly cat. I'm sure children will get a thrill and/or a nightmare when reading about him.

***

It is now ten years since we, I use the word loosely, *welcomed*, Max into our home.

"Have any of us had a full night's sleep in that time?" you may well ask.

"No!" said Ray, unable to sleep one night. "Fifty-seven screams, then he went quiet and gave up," he reported the following morning.

Do we love Maxi? Yes, we do, although the cat doesn't reward us for our love and care. Just looking at him, one would think butter wouldn't melt in his mouth.

"Have you noticed that Max and I have similar natures?" said Alice, "you can love us all you want, but we will not conform or return your love. It's just how we roll!"

Isn't that the truth? A cat with issues, just what we needed! Umm, I think I know why the cat was relinquished in the first place. The previous owners had no sense of adventure.

Chapter 40

A Celebration Of Harald's Life

"Karin, I have just told your sisters I want you to conduct my funeral," said Dad, trying to sound very matter of fact about this proposal.

"Gee, Dad, when do you think you might die?" I asked in a facetious manner.

"I just want to have everything arranged, so that everyone knows exactly what I want. Can you take some notes?" he asked.

With notebook and pen poised, I sat mesmerised, as he candidly discussed his life, his loves, his dreams, and his aspirations. Mum, who had been an avid raconteur, had repeatedly told us the same stories of his life. However, it was interesting to hear those identical stories from my father's perspective, and in his own voice. I didn't write anything down. I already knew this man.

Do you know Harald Lorek? You may have seen him sitting on the bench at the entry to Coles at the Mandurah Forum when he used to wait for his wife of 65 years to complete the weekly grocery shopping. If you noticed him at all, you may have thought he was just another elderly gentleman sitting there, as he had nothing better to do than watch the world go by. You may have thought he was in pain, as you noted that he was nursing a shonky knee or a stiff back. Perhaps he smiled cheekily at you and said good morning. A friendly old codger you may have thought.

Or did you recognise him as an older version of someone you once knew well, and thought *he looks a bit familiar, like the bloke, what's his name, yeh, that bloke from the Lions Club. Heck, is he still going? I remember him when he was the President of the Merredin Lions Club. He was president for several terms. He was honoured with a Life Membership of Lions International for 100% attendance over his 57 years with the club. Wonder what he's doing in Mandurah"* you may have thought.

Or do you recognise him from a church group where, over time, he not only carried out deacon roles, but also gave the odd sermon. *Gee, he's funny*, you'd think. Had a German accent and was forever laughing and joking (*yoking* as he would pronounce the word). He always made everyone feel special and most welcome. If it wasn't for Harald, most of the older ladies wouldn't have even got to church. He always was running a continual shuttle service back and forth. Talk about energy, he was into everything, and nothing was too much trouble for him. Never walked, he ran! His poor, long-suffering wife Anna would calmly put up with his shenanigans, dismissing it all with, "It's just Harald being Harald."

Talk about being adventurous! Even with his strong German accent, he was a founding member of the Merredin Rostrum Club. He could string a good set of words together, although sometimes members couldn't understand him, as his accent was too *thick* or *sick* as he would say. Some of his grammar wasn't correct English either. However, he was only speaking as he was translating from German, which ironically often gets lost in translation. Sometimes he would be killing himself laughing in his cheeky lively manner, and everyone else in the room would have that *think I must have missed something look* on their faces.

Do you remember him? Perhaps he's the guy with whom you used to play golf. Wow, talk about a hacker! He didn't walk the course, he ran it. They tried to tell him the game was supposed to last all afternoon, but Harald would quickly chip his way around the greens, or should one say *browns,* as was the golf course up there in Nokaning.

You may have seen him at the local library, as he browsed through the selection of thrillers. Goodness, he must be a voracious reader, you may have thought, as he staggered to the counter with another arm full of books. *Well, that'll take him to the rest of his days to read them.* But, sure enough, same time the next week, he could be seen collecting his weekly supply of new reading matter. In later years, his E-books were sent to his Kindle directly from the Mandurah Library.

Hey, that's the bloke who plays chess every week with his learned mates. Always on the lookout for opportunities to checkmate a new opponent. He'd invite streams of hopefuls, young and old, who fronted up to show him a thing or two about chess. Most often, that same stream of hopefuls would leave with their tail between their legs after a flogging.

"Who's next?" Harald would laugh.

Well, what he's doing in Mandurah? He lived in Merredin for 50 something years in the house he built with his own two hands. It was quite trendy for its time. Had big rooms, was beautifully decorated and, in years later, he was one of the first guys to put in a pool. Those lucky kids of his suddenly got heaps of new friends, as everyone wanted to go over for a swim. The house was built on a huge block, and eventually became surrounded by fruit trees, grape vines, vegetable patches, sheds, a massive rose garden, and a chook pen. For many years, there was even a horse in the back yard.

It's hard to believe the entire family lived in a shed the size of a garage, while the house was being built. The building program was interrupted, as Harald contracted Polio while in the process of his owner builder program. That disease was rampant in Australia in the mid to late 1950s. Anna, his wife, worked several jobs to make ends meet. It was all hands-on deck to nurse Harald back to good health, care for the home front, plus put food on the table. Even his incredibly young daughters had their job of caring for their father and sat by his bedside during the day to feed him, changing his sweat sodden pyjamas, and cooling his brow with iced towels.

Harald recalls the days when local tradespeople would gather at his building site offering to lend a hand.

"What would you like us to do?" they asked. Harald, physically weak from the effects of his illness, could just lay on an old wire bed nearby and, frustratingly for him, could only offer his moral support and humble appreciation.

Having no other family in Australia, it was a case of doing what was necessary to survive. Anna worked tirelessly at her cleaning job at the Bank of New South Wales, her waitress job at *Aunty Lisa and *Uncle Kasey's Ritz Cafe, and her ironing job at *Mummy Ivy's Laundry. (*Terms of endearment for blood relative substitutes)

After three years working as a farm labourer, Harald moved his family into the Merredin township, and found work with a house-building company. There he learnt the skills needed to build his own home. It was while he was negotiating the purchase of tiles for his house that the owner of the concrete factory offered him a job as his factory manager. However, his days of making roof tiles, slabs, and livestock troughs were cut short when he became sick with stomach ulcers. The doctor told him he should quit working with concrete, as this was the cause of his ill health.

Not long after that, the sounds of Harald's dulcet tones calling out *laundry"* became common place, as he delivered freshly laundered baskets of clothes and/or linen to their customers' homes or offices. Harald and Anna had embarked on their own business venture and had set up a modern commercial laundry in the town. Sheets, sheets, and more sheets came from everywhere. And then there were shirts, shirts, and more shirts for Anna to hand iron. Everyone said she was the best at ironing they had ever seen, and brought their linen tablecloths, formal lodge shirts, and damask serviettes for her to starch and iron up like new. The three daughters also had their ritual of daily duties which were totally non-negotiable.

Through this labour-intensive business, Harald and Anna earned the utmost respect in the town for their efficient service and became popular with clients and other business proprietors alike. Their strong work ethic, their can-do attitude, plus their commitment and participation in community affairs brought them many years of happiness and satisfaction.

That old friendly guy is the much loved and respected father of three daughters, grandfather of seven, great grandfather of seventeen, and great great grandfather of one.

Yes, time changes us all. From that tall dark and extremely handsome 23-year-old German migrant who rode into town on the back of a utility, seeking work as a farm hand all those years ago, to this kindly old gentleman, just sitting, patiently waiting, and happily smiling.

At 92 years of age, still living life to the fullest, Harald has earned his right to be riding his gopher at the Mandurah Forum. If you look very closely, past the white hair and the odd wrinkle, you will still see that same youthful sparkle in his eyes. It's not gone, nor is that mischievous smile, or his infectious sense of humour. He'll probably say *Gut morning* to you, and you'll note his strong German accent, something time still hasn't erased. He may compliment you on your lovely outfit, try to help you carry your load of groceries, or even attempt to tell you a joke, but bear with him, it may be a bit lost in translation.

You may remember him for one or many of the roles which he faithfully played throughout his long and fortunate life.

Daughters Anne, Gaby, and I just know him as our father.

In memory of Harald Lorek 18/11/1929 -22/12/2023

Chapter 41

A Trip Down Memory Lane

"Remember the old farmyard?" I asked Ray, as we sat reminiscing about the farm which he had known as his home, his playground, and his work for the first 36 years of his life.

"We had so many bloody chooks. They ran free all day, and we'd only locked them up at night to protect them from the foxes. Gee, if I had a dollar for every egg, I found in the wood heap and the haystacks, I'd be a rich man," he recollected.

"Yeah, I remember the ducks, and the shitty mess they made. I used to have to walk on my tippy toes to avoid getting muck on my white platform shoes," I laughed. I had never been one to dress appropriately for the farm.

In my mind's eye I could see the massive Lilac Tree in the centre of the yard. It had been everyone's shelter. The working dogs were chained up under it every night. The chooks sat on its branches by day, and the ducks congregated beneath its summer shade. Cockatoos, crows, and magpies also nested there; hence each family member wore a hat whenever they ventured anywhere near that hundred-year-old tree. The trotting horses in the nearby yard would pop their heads over the fence to get a closer checking at the prolific bird life. Collectively it appeared like a scene from a children's story book.

"I certainly don't miss milking the cow every morning and night," grunted Ray. His old-fashioned father insisted there be a cow always on-site. It was supposed to save us money on milk and cream. I don't think old Charlie even knew that milk and cream came in cartons, and the cost of keeping a cow, making up chaff every month, plus all the time and energy we'd put into the free milk operation, far outweighed the cost of buying a pint from the shop. He'd never even milked a cow. That job was left to Mum and the boys.

Ray stared into the air, and imagined the footprint of his size eight Blundstone boots that must surely still be embedded in the farmyard sandy tracks where he had once walked daily.

"Pity Dad was such a hoarder. Every time he went to a clearing sale or the local tip, he'd come back with boxes and boxes of sundries, *the stock company's official term for rubbish*. He reckoned it could all be useful one day."

Consequently, the yards and the sheds were overfilled to the brim with metal sundries: pieces of heavy chain, old horse and cart equipment, rusted tools, sheets of metal, and all that type of *handy stuff*. When a shed could no longer hold any more junk, Dad would insist the boys help him fashion up a new one. When that was full, another was built, and then another.

Okay, we Jarvises weren't fancy, but it was a working pioneer farm, a hive of activity, where there was always something happening: from farm vehicles coming and going, tractors being driven through the yards, sheep being herded towards the shearing shed, animal kills for domestic use, people visiting, and even six of the older grandchildren running around, dodging danger with every move.

It was now well over three decades since we had packed up our meagre possessions and, with our three children, headed off to Perth to seek a new life. A life where we planned to become the masters of our own destinies. A life where I could use my limited skills to earn money, and where Ray, as son number three, would not only be freed from the family pecking order, but would also be able to forge his own identity, and be autonomous in making his own life choices.

It was also 30 years since we had last set foot on the family home farm: the place Ray was born to, the land he had worked on every day for thirty-six years, the property he, as a younger man, had envisaged owning, the place he'd loved.

It was time to go back home!

As it was now owned by his elder brother, we first sought permission to enter. He had inherited the home farm after the death of their father some 30 years earlier. The middle brother inherited another farm which was situated just out of town, and Ray had freely signed over his land inheritance to them. He knew they were better equipped to farm, since he was now living in Perth, and besides, in his memory, farming had never been a financially viable proposition.

Turning into the property from the main road, we drove over a rickety wooden bridge, now severely white ant eaten, and held together by metal bolts, fencing wire, and a prayer. As we entered through the old farmyard gates, Ray and I glanced at each other in surprise. Is this the same farm? I noted his face portrayed a stoic mask, as he inwardly cringed with embarrassment and despair.

Gone were the birds, the horses, and the cow. Gone was that ancient Lilac Tree. Gone was any form of colour, or the hustle and bustle of farm life which we so vividly remembered. In its place was course red sand that had been well and truly sifted through by teams of marauding bull-ants, the only form of life in my line of sight. Around the perimeter of the yard were twisted shells of iron sheds, time and white ants having contributed towards their collapse, to fully entomb the decaying sundries that lay beneath. The wooden fence posts, which Ray and his brothers had cut by hand during their school holidays, lay crumbled to the ground, each resembling a small pile of wood chips. The fencing wires had been retrieved and added to the ever-growing heaps of rusty scrap metal. Tractors, combines, and ploughs, once fully functional, rested on their metal axles, rusted, barely recognisable.

Shapes and colours of grey decaying sheds, orange ochre rusted silos, black charred rubbish piles, and the red, bare surrounding land, stood in stark contrast against the light blue of the clear autumn sky. It was a scene that would have captured the imagination of Jolliffe, to use in his *Salt Bush Bill* cartoon series.

Once prime real estate, the vibrant, viable farm now lay dormant, appearing nothing more than a graveyard of a by-gone era. The culmination of drought, debt, ill health, and neglect had reduced this property to a hopeless burden, a hindrance to joy, and a deterrent to any future buyer.

All was quiet, except for the monotonous clanging of a loose corrugated iron sheet, which flapped in the light breeze. *The ghost of Charlie Jarvis*, I assumed.

"Okay, I've seen enough. Let's go," Ray said, breaking the sombre silence.

***

The story of Ray, his brothers, and the split up of the farming property is a sensitive one. One brother has since passed, and his estate underwent legal argument between his two next of kin long after his death.

The other brother was diagnosed with a life-threatening neurological illness, and soon after was unable to give his complete time and energy to running the property. That farm has since been sold.

Three brothers, all brought up to love the land, all with differing ideas on how this should be done, all marrying women of different personalities and all wanting the best for their own family.

If there's something I've learned from all my goodbyes and hellos, it's this: a mother will fight tooth and nail for her children, and a man will protect his territory until there is no more fight left in him. Each of the three brothers did what they believed to be right to protect their own livelihoods. Each family, including us, did their darndest to give their children the best life possible. Perhaps in hindsight, it could have been handled differently, but who knows? Truth be told, if the brothers had had the opportunity to write their recollection of the same events, all stories may differ, for reasons only known to them.

In Memory of Murray Jarvis 30/12/1947 -11/8/2022

Chapter 42

Where To From Here?

"Alice, I'm coming with you on your next Psychiatrist appointment. I'm planning to make a scene, so be prepared!"

"Gee, Mum, settle down. I don't need you making a fool of yourself. What's your problem anyway?"

"I'm sick of sending you to professionals who don't give a darn about you. First you are made to wait for months to get an appointment, and when you finally get there, they just write out a prescription for Class 1 drugs, take your money, and send you home for another six months. I thought psychiatry was all about helping people to resolve their issues. In the meantime, you hang about the house depressed, crying, too anxious to go out, too scared to venture to the shops, too petrified to even talk to a neighbour. You only communicate via the internet, you disrespect us, you do nothing around the house, and your only friends are the dog and the cat. For God's sake, I want bloody action! This has gone on for far too long, and I am getting bloody sick of it."

WOW, where's that coming from? I'd just thrown a complete mental, said what I really meant, and didn't spare the language.

***

"Hello, Mrs Jarvis, and how are you going Alice?" asked the delightful Psychiatrist.

As usual, Alice grunted, flinched her shoulders, and stared down at the floor.

I took charge of the conversation. "I'm here today to see what can be done for Alice. She's been coming here for years, and not once have you recommended a program for her. You've alluded to the fact she may have Asperger's. I have researched it, and I believe she has it.

"Yeah, I've always thought I've had that," Alice piped up.

"She definitely displays the behaviours, but I'm unable to officially diagnose her, and a true diagnosis would cost a lot of money," he replied.

I had gone there for action, and felt I had to be prepared for whatever the outcome. "What sort of money are we talking about?" I enquired, as I bit my tongue to prepare myself for the financial inevitable.

"A lot. It could run into thousands and thousands of dollars, and even then, you may or may not get a complete diagnosis. It's not covered on Medicare, so it would be your financial responsibility." At 34 years of age, Alice had been living life in the inescapable prison of her mind. Depression, anxiety, anger, negativity, loneliness, and lack of self-worth were her only constants. This was not the time to think about money. Anyway, why hadn't we had this conversation years before? I began to feel disappointed in myself for not having had an anger outburst years ago. *But weren't they the professionals? I thought they knew what they were doing. Who was I to tell them what to do? Didn't anyone else see the signs years ago? It's not like we haven't been visiting doctors and education professionals for years and years.* I felt the anger rise in my chest and was totally surprised at the calmness with which I answered.

"Okay, what do we do, where do we go, and when can we start?"

That conversation led to another doctor's visit, for a referral to the psychiatrist's recommended clinical psychologist 70 kilometres away in Applecross. Frustratingly, there was not one closer to our home in Mandurah. Appointments were made which were the prelude to six months of bi-weekly visits. Six months of testing, questionnaires, conversations, box ticking, and analysis of Alice and myself. They were not just taking my word for it. Was I just a bad mother, or was my daughter the genuine article?

As I observed Alice during her interviews and conversations, I could see the traits of Autism: lack of eye contact, disjointed sentences, lack of self-worth, lack of displays of affection, saying what she thought with absolutely no filter as to other's feelings. Particularly mine. She lacked concentration and sat curled up on the couch like a cat, changing positions every minute or so, totally oblivious to acceptable adult standards and protocols.

Well, the psychiatrist was correct, it did take a lot of money to fund these visits. However, despite me being no longer employed, and Alice only being on a Newstart Allowance, Ray and I agreed: Alice was our top priority. We would take the money from our meagre superannuation fund, set aside for our retirement.

***

"Okay, I've finished the testing now, and once you pay for the report, you will be able to take the next step," announced the agreeable young clinical psychologist with a smile.

"Pay for the report?" I asked.

"Yes, once you've put $1,500 into my account, I will start to write the report."

Considering we had been paying $500 per week for the testing, I was surprised at that request. But what was the testing without the report? Nothing! I reached for my credit card from my bag and proceeded to pay for the mysterious report. At this stage, Alice's condition was still unknown to us. The doctor did not give so much as a hint. Money first, then wait three months to receive the diagnoses, it seemed.

Exactly three months to the day from the final testing, we received a report via email stating that Alice had Type 2 Autism (high functioning autism known previously as Asperger's Syndrome) and would qualify for funding from the National Disability Scheme.

I cried for my beautiful daughter. She had endured the school system with obvious learning disabilities, social disabilities, mental disabilities, and behavioural issues, and not one professional had picked it up. I knew there was something not right with her when she was a tiny baby, and we had been shoved from pillar to post, put in the too hard basket, and ignored ever since. To say I felt angry is an understatement!

My heart goes out to parents of children who have found themselves in the same predicament as us. My thoughts and prayers are with the children, young people and adults who have been passed over by the education system, the medical system, and employers, all because they have not had an expensive diagnosis. I fear the prisons are packed with people with autism, ADHD, and similar disorders.

Where do we go from here?

It's amazing how life can improve once one has an official diagnosis on public record. At least my life has. I am at peace knowing that Alice has a condition which I have researched and is therefore not responsible for her behaviour. I endeavour to concentrate on all the artistic, creative, kind, and generous things she can do, and tend not to react when her autistic behaviours appear. "Thank goodness, about time!" she may say.

However, the diagnosis isn't a magic bullet for Alice. She still avoids new people, has anxiety, fears, phobias, and communicative problems, but at the very least, she knows she can't help it, and that's just the way things are for her. She knows she has value and worth as a human being. We encourage her to travel and explore, not only the world, but also her spiritual side. She enjoys yoga, sewing, music, design, animals, and loves to spend time researching her favourite interests.

And where to from here? God only knows!

Footnote: I'm no poet but recently felt moved to write the following:

ANOTHER $5,000

Born protesting. Screaming. Head banging. Anger in her eyes
Hold her. Feed her. Starve her. Drug her. Cuddles you should her deny
It's your baby, deal with it! Not our problem. A rod for your own back
Congrats on the new kid. Ha-ha! Not our fault, good parenting skills you lack

Insomnia. Strolls at midnight, pushing pram through wind and rain we walk
Please go to sleep, sweet child of ours. We weep. We sing. We talk
Slumber seldom comes. Anger lurks deep in this child so planned and loved
With tiredness and frustration comes temptation, this child to be shoved

Years pass. Still screaming. Head banging. Anger in her eyes. No change in behaviour
Help is sought: doctors, teachers, specialists, psychologists, prayer, seeking a saviour
We can help, each replies so clearly. Pay $5, 000 to my account, for testing to commence
Months observing, questionnaires, interviews, reports, all add to the expense

Thirty-five years of screaming. Head banging. Anger in her eyes. A potential suicide statistic
It's Dyslexia, ADHD, Depression, Asperger's, Borderline Personality, and finally: "No, she's Autistic!"
Dexamphetamine, antidepressants, hormones, therapy, counselling, all we must buy
As we grow older, our love for her strengthens, yet we ponder her future when <u>we</u> die

I cry for parents of babies born screaming, head banging, with anger in their eyes
Are they still alive today? Suicidal? On drugs? In the gutters? Has their freedom been denied?
"Vermin! Addicts! Get a job! We pay for these lazy bastards," write the trollers
Oh, where would my baby be today, if each time, we could not find another 5,000 dollars?

Chapter 43

The Entrapment Of Our Minds

The following are excerpts taken from Alice's Facebook page:

"Alice in Wonderland? Alice in Chains? Alice in the Palace? Who the f@#k is Alice?
Yeah, who the f@#k am I?
My own personal Blazing Swan experience was full of highs, moments of anxiety, and complete fear. I can get up in front of a crowd of people and DJ, dance, insult, MC Unicorn marches, play trashy guitars, and pretend I'm a rock star, but to walk into a crowd of people talking with one another is a complete shit storm in my brain.

If I did not speak with you, I'm sorry. I get shy, anxious, or I become blank. Unlike on Facebook, where words seem to flow out in typed format. Not always the most intelligent of ideas, but what else would you expect from a chick called Alice who is half unicorn and half cat, trying to have a human experience.

Fears and anxieties are all I have in my brain. Plus, I'm sick of being alone, but feel like I'm the biggest retard around people. I have nothing of worth to say, so I just end up talking about my cat, because I love him, but he is a deaf cat, and there's only so much other people can handle from me, especially if I just talk about cats. Plus, the way I type stuff is the way I talk, all these thoughts come out, and I forget that conversation is a two-way thing, and I go blank because I'm anxious, and I hate my own thoughts about anything."

****

Alice's comment to a Facebook post November 2020, during a discussion on why there are so many drug-affected youths in the area:
"Are they undiagnosed ADHD or high functioning autistic? Did their parents feed them unhealthy food? Do their parents lack emotional understanding, and refer to these children as selfish brats?
No one figured out I was ADHD until I was 17. Eventually at the age of 34, after I failed to thrive and keep up with my peers, I was diagnosed

with High Functioning Autism. Everyone just wrote me off as being disobedient, lazy, and emotional. However, I was so depressed, I could barely get out of bed. I felt as though my brain had just stopped functioning. I believe so many people in jails have not been given a fair chance by society and could have underlying issues. They are labelled as "pieces of rubbish" which further perpetuates their unsocial behaviour. It took me until the age of 36 to come to terms with myself and know that it is okay to be me. Please don't write off the troubled kids. They are the creative ones, and given the understanding and the opportunity, they will do amazing things in their own way.

Facebook post November 2020: "Allowing a student with a hidden disability (ADHD, Anxiety, Dyslexia) to struggle academically or socially when all that is needed for success are the appropriate accommodations and explicit instruction, is no different than failing to provide a ramp for a person in a wheelchair."

Alice's reply: *What a stuff-up my education was! But I guess they did not know any better back then. I have never been able to finish any structured education course. But that's okay, I'm not angry anymore. It was what it was.*

****

"My mum wrote about me on the Internet. Below is what I copied and pasted. Lol!" 32 years ago, I gave birth to an Indigo Child. Over the years I treated her as though she was a punishment from above because she was so unlike my other *normal* children. Okay, it was tough! (understatement).

My efforts to understand her led me to many gurus, church leaders, exorcism meetings, medical specialists, hypnotists, naturopaths, psychiatrists, education specialists, the list went on and on. All were happy to take the money of a desperate mother searching for answers. No help was found!

I finally started to listen to my child, slow learner that I am, 32 years later. She spoke to me about healing foods, creative pursuits, love for fellow human beings, acceptance of all, even social outcasts! She speaks of other realms, of energies from beyond, dreams, astral travel, yoga, health, and meditation. She enlightened me about YouTube: Channelling

Erik, Channelling Jesus, Alien forces, Facebook, free thinking, and the need for society to wake up.

I was so under the impression that the frustration was mine: trying to wake up this beautiful person so she could have the normal life I have lived. Yep, she too should chase her tail every day trying to make ends meet, endure obligatory relationships, and inherit fake beliefs which have been handed down from generation to generation. She too should believe everything I told her, just because that was my reality. To be just like me: a nervous wreck. Yep, she too could enjoy *the good life,* if she were only to conform to my belief system.

What a frustrating life she must have had, to be born to a mother like me. Finally, I stopped work, quietened my mind, and listened to her. Better late than never! For the first time in my life, I started to see clearly.

I thank the universe for my daughter. How blessed am I to have my teacher walking with me through life? I have so much happiness, love, and thankfulness in my heart, I could cry with joy. Alice, I am learning so much from you, at your insistence. My dull mind is awakening. Thank you so much. Light and love to you, my darling.

Chapter 44

Labels, Acronyms, Reality

Dyslexia: a reading disorder, characterised by trouble with reading, despite normal intelligence. Problems include difficulties in spelling words, reading quickly, writing words, sounding out words in the head, pronouncing words when reading aloud, and understanding what one reads. The difficulties are involuntary, and people with this disorder have a normal desire to learn. Can run in families. It often occurs in people with attention deficit hyperactivity disorder (ADHD).

Attention Deficit Hyperactivity Disorder: a neurodevelopmental mental disorder, characterised by difficulty paying attention, excessive activity, and behaviour without regards to consequences, which are otherwise not appropriate for a person's age. Often problems with regulation of emotions, etc, and the list goes on.

Depression: A mental health disorder characterised by persistently depressed mood or loss of interest in activities, causing significant impairment in daily life.

Autism Type 2 (Asperger's Syndrome) Challenges and difficulties with problem solving, making predictions, using high-level verbal reasoning skills, participating in general conversations including small talk, seeing and understanding others' viewpoints, empathising with others' feelings and emotions, tendency to become stressed when routines are altered, bundles of anxiety, problems with social skills, highly sensitive to sensory information, i.e. light, sound, texture and taste.

Diagnoses on a medical form, definitions sourced from Wikipedia, explanations for a mother, heavy chains to further shackle the sufferer for life.

As I transcribe the above, I am momentarily hit with a bout of self-pity, rage. My 36year-old daughter had openly displayed every one of the above *in your face* symptoms since birth, and not one professional in the medical or educational fraternity picked up on it, until this mother angrily came out swinging with her cheque book.

Autism Type 2, the latest label added to the suite of tags which adequately describes the symptoms of a nonconformist. However, with this very diagnosis, the government offered help in the form of a disability pension and NDIS qualification, with the hope she will live out her life and not be a menace to society's conformists.

Fancy acronyms and clever catch phrases are now part of our everyday language. Centrelink, NDIS, Kern Health, Enable, At Work, Match Works, and Peel Volunteer, all funded to fall over each other as they use their prescribed government financial allocation to offer Alice amenities and support never afforded her. For each entity to retain their budget, they must offer services and document outcomes. It appears Alice has personally created an industry for employment in the region for support workers.

However, does it fix anything? It saddens me to say, "No!"

I quieten my mind and allow myself to dream. I imagine a land where children and adults are permitted to be free spirits, where sleep is on a needs basis and not governed by a clock. I imagine a world where every person is given permission to use their own god given gifts and talents to carve out a life for themselves. Artists, authors, scientists, and all members of society are in sync with who they really are.

Where education is not about exams. Where sport is not about winning. Where curriculum is thrown out the window, as every child is encouraged to develop their own innate talents. Imagine! Where games are played for laughs. Where learning is enjoyed for the sake of gaining skills. I imagine a place where it's not mandatory to sit, stand, eat, or work on demand. Where sleeping in a bed or under the stars is a choice.

Where kids can be kids, and that zest for life is permitted to be carried into their adulthood with no reproach. Where all can laugh if they find something funny, and cry when they need to. Where the words "grow up" refer to a life process, not a derogatory command. Where people may be busy if desired, quiet if preferred, high-spirited if that mood arises. I imagine a place where inhabitants dress according to their own individual style and are not pressured to conform.

I imagine a world full of happy laughing people, a world where anxiety and fear are not even words found in the dictionary. Where creative energy is encouraged, and not suppressed. Where citizens are not pigeonholed, categorised, and thoughts muted. Imagine if inhabitants were not dictated to by the government, the social engineers, the glitterati, or the Illuminati?

"You're thinking about a primitive tribe. The reality is that we're civilised now. Those kids are feral, hippies, misfits of society," I hear you say.

But how happy would they be? In western culture, we label nonconformists as sick. They are snubbed by society. We hide them in mental institutions. Often, they are incarcerated.

Is it Alice who is awake, and me who is asleep? I believe Alice came to this world awake. She tells me it's time for me to wake up, to start living as my inner spirit intended me to. In our society, many call this mode of living "retirement," past our use-by date, the only opportunity most of us will ever get to living a life of our own choosing.

"You know what Alice? I think I get you!"

Chapter 45

A Man Or A Monk?

"It's cold enough to freeze the balls off a brass monkey here in Adelaide," wrote Ed, a prolific contributor to the spiritual Facebook group I followed.

I'm no keyboard warrior, and seldom feel the need to comment on anyone's posts, yet I responded. "Come west young man, come west." Over the many months of my membership to the Facebook page, I'd noted that Ed was one to comment wisely and confidently on almost every one of the author's posts. I also noted that he was Australian and would know that Perth winters were obviously so much warmer. I believed I had bragging rights.

To my surprise Ed responded to my comment and asked if I'd read any books by an author named Tina Spalding. I had already purchased and read most of her books. A conversation about the contents of those volumes ensured. The chats continued via messenger. He sent me regular updates on YouTube podcasts by that author. We discussed in depth our favourite passages in each book and shared our passion for subjects pertaining to spiritual matters. We both agreed that our favourite spiritual master was Jesus. And our favourite book was *Jesus, My Autobiography*.

I loved our written conversations and would eagerly await the next instalment of enlightenment. These are the chats I loved to have. However, most people I knew were either not on a spiritual path or had been indoctrinated by religion in their childhood and refused to explore further. Therefore, it was difficult to discuss matters which could open their minds, add to their joy, or even give them peace of mind, body, and soul. Alice had often spoken of these wonders, and now I was hearing it from a quieter, calmer and a more eloquent voice. I had learnt much about spirituality during my years of practising Christianity. However now I was learning to listen to God, to the universe, to mother earth and not to mankind.

My alone time was becoming obvious to my family. I'd stay in my room until I was summonsed to attend our 5 o'clock drinks each evening. I'd read my books, listen to spiritual podcasts, write in my journal, and meditate. I was learning so much about God, the universe, good health, healthy minds, and the list went on. I'd check in with Ed from time to time as he'd confirm my findings and share his journey with me. These communications endured for over three months.

"I'm coming to Perth to cat-sit in Bunbury. I'll have six days in Perth before I head down south." Ed wrote.

"Okay, you can stay at my place," I blurted out, before even asking Ray for his approval.

Wow, now I was going to meet this peaceful, loving, intelligent soul. The one who is on a strict spiritual path. The one who is so health conscious, he refuses to eat foods that don't nourish his body. He doesn't drink alcohol. He exercises daily, meditates, and leads a life he believes is honouring to God.

This guy sounded like a monk. I felt like a fraud. *Goodness, am I going to have to pretend to be all goody-two-shoes? How does one give up alcohol, sugar, chocolate, and all the naughty stuff I've been consuming all my life? Do I pretend that I am more spiritual than I am?*

Ray's and Alice's reaction to Ed's impending visit was not enthusiastic, to say the least. Ray had seen him as a threat to himself, thinking I may have more in common with my new male friend than I had with him. My husband had always told people that I was attracted to spiritual people, however he always said it with an air of disdain.

True to form, Alice just hated visitors in the house. Her condition of Autism 2 (Aspergers) meant that she didn't welcome new people into her space at all. She had always verbally abused me when I invited friends to our home.

"Why did you invite people here again. I hate people coming to the house. You always clean the house and make me clean my bathroom," she would express as an accusation.

However, this time, she felt trouble looming. Her anxiety was obvious. She begged me to renege on my invitation to Ed. But I'd given my word, and I wanted to honour that. Besides, I was going to meet a like-minded soul, even though my eating, drinking and spiritual habits were not as saintly as his. It was going to be interesting to meet a person with common interests.

Ed and I enjoyed each other's company at first meeting. We chatted animatedly all the way home from the airport. I listened intently as he explained his clean eating regime. *Goodness, I've never heard of all the stuff he eats. I wonder if Coles even stocks it. What the heck is Filmjolk Probiotic Yoghurt? What is Hemp Seed and where do I buy free-range eggs laid by hens that aren't packed in under 1500 per hectare?*

Our trip to the supermarket turned into an educational for me; where to find the products that would nourish each cell in the human body. He led me past all my usual grocery aisles and introduced me to wild caught salmon, organic sauces, free-range and grass-fed meats, probiotic dairy, Kombucha and products without added sugars. He read all package labels, evaluated the ratio of dollars per gram, and assessed the best value of all products. Processed foods were rejected. Instead, the trolly was loaded with nuts, seeds, organic, natural, and sugarless ingredients. I listened with great interest. Here was a man in his late 50s with the body of a 25-year-old athlete. He was tall, slim, and strong. He mentioned he hadn't visited a doctor in years. He had never caught a cold, not even the dreaded Covid since he discovered this alternative healthy lifestyle. Ed's mantra was, "Let food be your medicine and let medicine be your food." A quote borrowed from Hippocrates, the father of modern medicine. His wish was to help people shed kilos which would lead them to a healthier, happier life.

It was time for this 68-year-old woman, carrying an excess of 20 kilos, to be alert, to shut up and listen.

Food preparation was another eye-opener as he introduced me to simple cooking with coconut oil. He did use butter but very sparingly. However, at no time did I feel he was forcing me to change my ways. He'd often say,

"You may wish to rethink your options."

Seriously, the only thing I had to gain was good health and the only thing I had to lose was 20 kilos. Now, why wouldn't I have a rethink?

Alice had often said that she suffered food allergies and gut issues. I had no idea if she was just being a drama queen, as she usually gave negative critiques on my cooking after every meal. It never occurred to me to change my style of cooking just to please her. In hindsight, my own health wasn't exactly exemplary. My daily alcohol routine and my love of sugar products and high carbohydrate foods may be the eventual death of me.

Ed explained, "We are all responsible for our own health. We can't continue to live our sedentary western lifestyle without it taking a toll on our bodies." He said that most people are slowly committing suicide just by their food choices.

Which rock had I been hiding under for all those years? Why didn't I know this stuff? What had I been doing to my entire family? I couldn't do anything about the past. However, armed with this newfound knowledge, I could change the future. It was up to me.

Evening entertainment also brought another challenge. Ed refused to watch television. He felt that the newscasts brought only orchestrated fear into each household and was contributing to peoples' negative thinking, and even depression. As an alternative to the evenings viewing, Ed suggested we search some YouTube channels to check out various spiritual masters, or listen to Tina Spalding's videos "Channelling Jesus."[10]

"Far more uplifting and enlightening than watching a television series peppered with death, fighting, misunderstandings, and all things undesirable," he said. I agreed. Ray chose to watch commercial television while Ed and I headed for my computer where we settled into an evening of uplifting enlightenment and thought-provoking discussions.

Was I just infatuated by this tall, fit, intelligent, energetic stranger? My family thought so. But I felt alive. I sensed I was finally on the right path to discover the life I wanted to live. Even though I had followed the Christian faith for so many years, I found it to be a doctrine of fear, of hierarchy, with the bar being set to unachievable heights. I tried so often and had failed equally as often.

Ray remarked that I was like an impressionable schoolgirl, hanging onto Ed's every word. However, my new friend and my common interests may have brought us together, but my passion and thirst for further knowledge in spiritual matters and intelligent conversation had always been of the upmost interest to me long before our meeting. As they say, "When the student is ready, the teacher will appear," and I was more than ready to change my health status, my spiritual outlook, and

---

[10] *Channelling Jesus* videos available on YouTube, channelled by trans-channel and author Tina Spalding

all aspects of my personal life. Finally, I believed this was my time and I was going to make the best of it. I loved to learn, and the world was my classroom. *Bring it on!*

Being an avid reader, Ed had at least six nonfiction books on the go at any one time. He was a font of knowledge and shared facts from each of his current E-books. Such wisdom and passion I had never heard from anyone.

"No, I'm not super special. I'm just a man with a high aptitude for learning and a desire to live life consciously," he'd say. "If you really want to make changes in your life, you can. In the words of Paulo Coelho, "And one day I understood that it's no one's job but mine, to take care of myself and make myself happy." If you want to make changes, you must have the faith and the courage to change.

I had the faith, but did I have the courage?

Ed left our home after six days. Ray was pleased to be rid of him as he had witnessed me changing before his eyes. Alice was pleased to see the back of him too. She had perceived a threat before his arrival, and now, her intuition was proving to be correct. She sensed she was losing her mother. Her world was changing. Fear, anger, and anxiety was setting in.

And it was true, I would never be the same person again.

Chapter 46

Happy 50th Wedding Anniversary

"This didn't make you happy!" screamed Alice, as she hurled a glass bowl of hand-crafted silk orchids across the room. "And this didn't make you happy!" She continued to unleash her anger on me as she blindly went from treasure to treasure, the ornaments of beauty I'd bought to enhance my home, my sanctuary, furiously smashing them on the floor. I stood there in absolute disbelief as my possessions were one by one been destroyed beyond repair.

"These are all fake and so are you." Tears of rage streamed from her eyes as she continued to leap like a wild animal from prey to prey. Her face contorted with anger as she continued to work herself up to a crescendo of absolute hate for me. I stood there in fear as I watched on in horror, subconsciously adding up the cost of her frenzied rampage. The home I loved, the home I'd worked almost seven days a week to pay for, the possessions I had purchased with an artistic eye to decorate my domain, my haven, were slowly being destroyed before my very eyes.

Ray and I could only watch on in fear as the rampage continued. Profanities directed at me accompanied each powerful throw. We couldn't reason with her. We knew her. When she was in a hysterical state, there was nothing we could do to calm her down. I knew my life could be in danger if I confronted her physically.

Next stop was my ensuite bathroom where she ruthlessly pulled out the drawers containing my makeup and face products, hurling each of them onto the floor tiles. Lotions, potions, glass items, eye shadows and lipsticks lay splattered and shattered on the floor. The once plain tiles now a kaleidoscope of chaos.

"Fake, all fake. These didn't make you happy. Nothing has ever made you happy. You've been living a lie. You're just so fake!" she shrieked.

Was she right? Had I been living a lie? Or had I just been keeping everyone else happy?

***

How time flies. Our 50th wedding anniversary had come and gone without so much of a word of congratulation from our three children or even a word from Ray. I certainly didn't initiate the subject. My dad and my sisters did phone and asked if Ray was taking me out on the town on this milestone occasion.

"I doubt it," I bluntly replied.

I'd always lived in hope that Ray would surprise me with a reservation at a restaurant for a special meal out, a surprise thoughtful gift (not alcohol) or even a simple card containing beautiful thoughtful words. However, over the 50 years, Ray was never one to surprise me with his initiatives, with words of love or gestures of affection. I was the driving force in the marriage and if I wanted something, I would need to come up with the idea, buy it or arrange it myself. I was tired of it.

"Ray, do you realise that yesterday was our 50th wedding anniversary?" I hesitated to ask, as we settled into our usual 5.00pm wine drinking session the following afternoon.

"Yes, I know. I also know that you don't like celebrating anniversaries," he replied, as if to absolve himself of any forgetfulness.

"And have you ever asked yourself, or me, why I don't like celebrating?" I questioned. *My goodness, I've got to get it out. I have to say something. This can't go on. I can't do this anymore. I'm done.*

Then unexpectedly, like I'd momentarily lost all self-control of my speech, my mouth opened and unrehearsed words just flowed.

"Ray, I haven't wanted to celebrate a wedding anniversary for so many years now as I can't believe that I'm still here. Whenever 21st October comes around, I hate myself for not having the courage to move on. I need to find myself as the person I came to Earth to be. I don't know who I am. I've been someone's daughter, mother, wife, and grandmother. I don't know who the heck I am. I don't even know what I like or what I believe. I know nothing. I don't even know what love is, short of being responsible for everyone around me and making sure their lives are ticking along nicely. I want to feel special. I want to feel love. I think we should release each other to go and find out who we are."

There I've said it. I stopped talking to digest what I had just blurted out. In retrospect, I had said the same words on so many occasions over the past 50 years. Now I'm saying them again. Will I let him talk me out of my dreams, again, just as I allowed him to do so many times before.

"No, we can work it out" he cried. "We've done it before; we can do it again."

"But we keep coming back to the same place. I can't keep doing this. I refuse to keep pretending that I'm happy when my heart is screaming out with frustration. I'm living a life that is suffocating me. Besides the kids and our assets, I don't think we even have anything in common. I hate talking about sport, the weather and whatever you've heard on talk-back radio. I'm into expanding my spiritual path. I love to read. I love to learn. I love to talk about spiritual matters. I love to write. I love to sing. I love to dance. I love to let my imagination run wild. I love different, even weird people. I do care about the environment. I don't want to kill spiders. I don't want to use poisonous substances about the house. I don't want my life to revolve around drinking alcohol every day at 5.00pm as we slowly kill our bodies. I want to evolve. I don't want to grow old knowing that I didn't have the guts to step away from a lifestyle that is not serving me. No, I must go. It's time to change."

"Okay, where are you going? You're 68, you won't have any money. You won't be able to get a job. You won't be able to fend for yourself."

"I don't know where I'll go. I've given this no thought. All I know is that if I don't change my life now, I may as well not live at all. I refuse to sit around and wait to die."

Suddenly, a loud human scream filled the air, followed by the sound of crashing objects. We ran into the living area to determine the source of the invasive noise.

There was Alice, radiating absolute fury, now with a $400 large glass vase overflowing with fake orchids in her hands, and proceeded to toss it across the room. She'd been listening to our conversation, and this was her reaction.

***

Verbal abuse of the most colourful and vulgar standard was being hurled at me as she expressed her disgust of me for suggesting that I should want a life apart from what was on offer here.

The pillage was not yet complete as she frantically sought further opportunities to ruin the beautiful home I'd contributed to for the family's use and pleasure.

"Ray, I can't live like this. This is not my home anymore. I must go now." I retreated to my room, grabbed a suitcase, and threw in several days' supply of clothes and some salvaged cosmetics from the bathroom floor. I grabbed my laptop, which Ray had seconds before prised out of Alice's hands as she threatened to smash it. I searched for my new reading glasses, but it was too late. She had already broken them in two. I headed towards my car. My dog Poppy, traumatised with all the screaming and smashing, ran to me for comfort. I couldn't weaken now. I forced myself to step over my dearest dog, the love of my life, and flee, immediately, if I wanted to survive my daughter's threats of further destruction to the house and to myself.

Ray waited near the car. Tears welling. He was biting his lip as he tried to hold in his emotions, utter despair written all over his face. I had just recaptured that familiar face of pain and hopelessness; I knew that grimace of anguish, and I hated inflicting it on him. I'd spent most of my married life trying to shield him from that pain. Consequently, I'd buried my own needs over so many years. Deep down, I believe he knew this day would come but had assumed I'd be too weak to carry through, or that he would be able to talk me out of it…again.

I briefly hugged Ray goodbye and drove off down the road to a future unknown. That house I had once loved was not my home anymore.

Goodbye beautiful home. Goodbye to a life that was smothering me. Goodbye to all I had known over the past 50 years.

Chapter 47

The Sisterhood

"Dear Valued friend.

Just to give you the heads-up. I'm seriously thinking of leaving Ray. I know, shock! Tomorrow is our 50th wedding anniversary and I really can't face another year of living a lie. I believe it's time for me to take responsibility for that. I love and value Ray as a person, but we don't share any common interests. We are not on the same page with our views on life and we don't respect each other's values. And what's more, we never laugh.

To be totally fair, he needs someone who he can enjoy his interests with i.e. sport, and that person is not me. I feel like a complete fraud as I half listen to his nightly rambling about football, cricket, what's on the television news and how thrilled his client is with the pressure cleaning job he did that day. To cope, I just keep drinking Chardonnay to survive the, ironically named, Happy Hour each night. He never asks me of my views, as he knows I'd take the conversation off onto a different tangent and he'd be lost, bored or would end up needing yet another alcoholic drink.

I know if it's going to be, it's up to me. I don't even know how I'll do it. God knows I've tried on so many occasions over the years. And no, there isn't another man I'm romantically involved with, although I'm feeling very inspired to change my life completely thanks to a special friend who's opened my eyes to a whole new world. Okay, love me, hate me, judge me. I'm okay with whatever you decide. I'll love you anyway."

I wrote to nine of my closest friends. Five of whom chose to positively embrace me. I refer to this group as *The Sisterhood*. Four, out of loyalty to Ray, or perhaps because I wasn't conducting my life in accordance with their standards and beliefs, chose to avoid me.

***

I finally did it! I'm out of that house and I'm driving to a destination unknown. To a life unknown, to a future unknown. I cast my mind back to 1985 to the time I had left my young family in Merredin to commence a life in real-estate, to lay the groundwork for a better life for them. I'd achieved that.

The older two kids, both parents, were living independently and thriving in their chosen fields. Alice, living at home at the age of 38, although high functioning, was still dependant on Ray and me. Try as I may, it was a challenge to teach her to take responsibility for herself. She was very capable of self-care but used her diagnoses as an excuse for not trying. I'm sorry, but I've given you the best years of my life Alice.

It's my turn now. I've been doing this since I was 18 and now, I'm done!

I knew Ray had the support of our son and daughters, his own siblings, my sisters, and my father as well. Plus, he had a beautiful spacious home, no debt, and a successful business to occupy his time. We agreed that I would continue to assist him with the running of the business bookwork. I would eventually move into our investment property once the tenants had vacated, within six months.

This time, as I drove from my family home, I wasn't sobbing with grief. This time I felt a wave of relief wash over my body. I was free. I had broken the chains that had held me back all my life. I'd been a people pleaser and had placed everyone's happiness and wellbeing before my own. Today, I, for the first time in my life gave myself permission to plan a future for myself.

"A future?" scoffed my 92-year-old dad. "You're 68 years old. You're nearly dead. Couldn't you just go along with the charade and keep everyone happy?"

"Dad, I understand your disappointment, but I can't live the life that you want for me. I can't even wait until you die before I try to find myself. I've kept everyone happy but me. Thats not the way anyone should live their lives." *Goodness, if I survived to be his age, I'd have another 24 years left on the planet. Surely, I had the right to live my life on my terms during the remainder of my time?*

It was no use discussing this with people who hadn't been through this situation before. They had their views as to why they stayed in a less than satisfactory marriage and I had mine. I was on my own. My family were in shock and chose to keep their distance from me. My only allies were the sisterhood and Ed. These friends had been through a separation themselves. They knew the pain. They knew what it was like to be shunned by family and friends. They knew loneliness and financial fears. The sisterhood were open-minded and non-judgemental. I felt comforted by them as they rallied to support me, provided a roof over my head, fed me, encouraged me, and listened as I justified my decision. They provided the tissues when I cried. None powered me with alcohol.

My first stop was to talk to Ed in Bunbury. He himself lived a nomadic lifestyle of pet sitting throughout Australia while he offered health coaching and worked on websites. He suggested I join a pet sitting website as a means of finding temporary accommodation while awaiting my own home to become available.

To my surprise, once the word was out, the requests and opportunities flowed in. Between the sisterhood and my pet sitting gigs, I was never without accommodation, and I was never without faithful friends who encouraged me throughout that time. I won't go into detail about the packing-up my possessions and my manic house cleaning (in true German hausfrau style) every 3 weeks, as thankfully that is now just a distant memory. I was simply happy to have had such beautiful homes to live in and gorgeous pets to keep me company.

***

For those of you who may be wondering if there was a romantic bond between Ed and myself, I will tell you as I've chosen to make this book an honest account of my hello-goodbye journey. After I left home, Ed and I fell into a fleeting romantic relationship. However, my perception was that he never felt comfortable about it. He was always holding back, and I sensed his mind was on higher matters. I also conceded that I was not ready for a new relationship as I hadn't yet grieved my last one. Fortunately, our shared interests and values were stronger than ever, so we agreed to resume our relationship as the best of friends. We proved that ex-lovers (however brief that liaison) can be friends and we both feel the richer for having had that experience. Our companionship has gone from strength to strength. We even encourage each other to explore new relationships if the opportunity should arise.

"You can't own another person and you can't chain a soul," we agreed.

Chapter 48

Check Point

"Sorry Val, can't talk, I'm on a roll, writing the last chapter of my book."

"I don't know how you can write the last chapter of your life story when the last episode of your life hasn't happened yet, and won't happen for a few years, at least, hopefully," corrected my very practical octogenarian friend from Scribblers. "Why are you even bothering to write it anyway?"

"My story is not exactly a linear account of my life, like a biography. It's a memoir about challenge, resilience, problem solving, patience, searching, with heaps of love and understanding thrown into the mix. Through my experiences, I see my story can be a catalyst for helping my reader understand that they too have choices. They can choose to love, or they can choose to hate. They can choose to blame, or they can choose to forgive. We can choose to go along with the status quo, or we can change our minds. We all have choice as we arrive at the crossroads of our life."

"Don't know how you survived it." she mused.

"Strange as it may sound Val, I was never alone on my journey, even though from time to time I did briefly feel abandoned. However, I always felt I had physical and/or non-physical beings guiding me along my path. For this I am most grateful." I explained, thinking my fellow writing colleague knew enough about my life to agree I could be an authority on my literary ability and my spiritual nature to share my story. "I think I've learnt enough to put pen to paper for my conclusion."

"Oh, I thought it was your life story, and if it's only part of it, so how can you conclude it?"

Let it rest, dear woman. She was becoming like a *dog with a bone.* However, she was quite right. The story does cover my life to date. However, from what I've learnt along the way, today I'll stop, reflect, and write a plan for the life I now choose for myself. Okay, let's just title this chapter *Check Point.*

As I write, I have been living alone in my new home for 12 months, the investment property which I have *Karinised*, a depiction used by people who know me well as they describe my house. It's brimming with indoor plants. The décor is coordinated, it's light and bright, minimalist in possessions and reflects my love of nature and clean spaces. I want for nothing. I have a part time job and have a whole new set of interesting colleagues, friends, and neighbours. I lost that excess 20kgs and am looking and feeling better than I have felt for many years. I remain on my diet of eating only enriching foods, stick to my regime of intermittent fasting and rarely drink alcohol. My spiritual path is my priority and daily journaling keeps me on track.

The sisterhood are still among my most loved friends, and Ed stays with me between his cat sits, in his own room. Ray visits from time to time and offers help with the heavy lifting and house maintenance. We will always be friends, however, the conversations have not changed. He still tells me about his work, laments over negative television news, and excitedly tells me about his lawn bowls, which he started after my departure. I enquire after Alice, Poppy the dog and Max the cat; my three loves who I haven't seen since leaving. I listen intently and wait for him to ask me a question on how I'm coping. He never does. Then I recall, he never has asked me that question over our 50 years of history. Nonetheless I'll forever welcome him to my home and show interest in his life. Divorce is an option for the future, but for now I know my freedom has caused him emotional pain and I don't wish to impose financial pain on him as well.

Two of our children have their own issues with our separation and I can only hope and pray that they will heal and forgive me for this disruption to their lives. I'm at peace with my decision, and I respect their choices.

***

Anyway, how am I going so far?

Was I brave enough to say goodbye? Now, that's debatable! On reflection, I recall a dash of foolhardiness, a smidgen of bravery, a truck load of tenacity, heaps of resilience, and the rest was sheer desperation. I mean who in their right mind leaves their babies to carry out reconnaissance for a whole new life? Who puts up with every form of bullying, abuse, and hardship to pursue a dream of giving her children every opportunity to become the best they can be? Who eventually leaves their marriage after 50 years to find themselves?

Who so often nearly blew the lot? Who fought back from every blow to rest, cry, and then get back out there again? My goodness, that desperado was me!

However, I never felt alone. I did meet angels at every crossroad to point me in the right direction. Some walked with me for a long or just a short distance on my journey. Some were nameless. Some were well meaning friends. Some may just have been figments of my imagination, my inner guidance or merely my intuition.

I thank Ray for walking with me for 50 years of my journey. I truly value his support and patience during that time. Ray's own life story can be likened to the renowned Aesop's fable, *The Tortoise and the Hare*, where the good guy eventually triumphed through his own courage, steadfastness, humility, and his never-give-up attitude. Despite his initial protestations, Ray has also grown.

However, I now choose to walk solo to find my authentic self. No lies, no pretence, no dependency and no settling for people or situations that do not add joy, peace, or love to my life.

So where do I go from here? I walk on knowing I have learnt the difference between holding a hand and chaining a soul. I know that company, partnership, or well-meaning advice does not mean security. Kisses between lovers or friends are not contracts, and can be voided, particularly when the going gets tough. Presents are not promises as I found they come with conditions. I've made mistakes along the way but own them as my lessons. I feel no shame or self-condemnation. It happened. I hold my head high. I am not defeated.

My plan from this day onwards is to build all my roads on today because tomorrow's ground is too uncertain for plans, and futures have a way of falling in mid-flight. I continue to plant my own garden and to decorate my own soul, instead of waiting for someone to bring me flowers, because I really am strong, I really can endure, and I really do have worth.

With every goodbye, I've learnt.

However, for now, this is not goodbye, it's auf wiedersehen!

Acknowledgements

Thank you, Veronica Shoffstall, without whom I may never have had the courage to say Goodbye.

Comes the Dawn

(Veronica Shoffstall)

After a while you learn the subtle difference
between holding a hand and chaining a soul,
and you learn that love doesn't mean leaning
and that company doesn't mean security,
and you begin to learn that kisses aren't
contracts, and presents aren't promises,
and you begin to accept your defeats
with your head up and your eyes open,
with the grace of a Woman,
not the grief of a child,
and you learn to build all your roads
on today because tomorrow's ground
is too uncertain for plans, and futures have
a way of falling down in mid-flight.
After a while you learn that even sunshine
burns if you get too much.
So, you plant your own garden and decorate
your own soul, instead of waiting
for someone to bring you flowers.
And you learn that you really can endure
and you really are strong
and you really do have worth.
And you learn and learn...
With every good-bye, you learn.

Thank you, *Scribblers Mandurah/Murray*. To Christine Elliott, Shirley Rowland and fellow members who critiqued my work and encouraged me to keep going. With extra special thanks to Lyn Tolliday for your encouragement, your editing expertise and especially for your friendship which I value.

Thank you to my beta readers/writing confidants: Lyn Tolliday, Ed Love, Peter Keil, Wade Zaglas, Jennifer Watt, Jennifer Marr, Lisa Kelly and Yvonne Stone: your comments, corrections, and suggestions are deeply appreciated.

Recommended Resources

Coelho, Paulo *"The Alchemist,"* HarperOne, USA. 2006

Lao-Tzu and Professor Lionel Giles (Translator). *"The Sayings of Lao Tzu-1904,"* Kessinger Publishing, USA. 2010

Love, Ed. *"The All You Can Eat Love Diet,"* www.edlovecoaching.com/love-diet/ Australia. 2004

Medhus, Elisa. *"My Life After Death, A Memoir from Heaven,"* Beyond Words. USA. 2015

Spalding, Tina Louise (Channelled). *"Jesus: My Autobiography,"* Light Technology Publishing. USA. 2015

Tolle, Eckhart. *"The Power of Now,"* Namaste Publishing, Vancouver Canada, 1997

About The Author

Karin Jarvis is a talented author, speaker, funeral celebrant and real estate professional. As a gifted writer, her love of the written word has provided her with countless opportunities to share her message, spread her wings and walk the road less travelled in life. However, Karin's path hasn't always been this way. Born to an immigrant family from Germany who settled in Merredin, Western Australia after the end of WW2, she grew up in the challenging environment of this small 1950s country town.

Despite her humble beginning working in her family's commercial laundry business, Karin yearned to create a better life for her young family. Choosing to pursue a career in Perth's burgeoning real estate industry of the 1980s, she left her small-town existence for the city and never looked back. As she met every challenge along the way, her motto became, *"With Every Goodbye You Learn."*

As a top performing real estate professional, Karin's qualifications include certification in Training and Assessment, Public Relations, Residential Property Management, Real Estate Sales, Funeral Celebrancy, and as a specialist Carer.

She has travelled extensively throughout Australia and the world, particularly Germany, Southeast Asia, United Kingdom, and the USA. Karin is also a mother of three adult children, and grandmother to four much-loved grandchildren. She still lives in the beautiful coastal city of Perth Western Australia, where she enjoys life to the full.

Contact The Author

If you would like to learn more about Karin's inspirational journey, latest writings, speaking availability and all book related news, please reach out to her at:

Email - karin@witheverygoodbye.com

Website - https://www.witheverygoodbye.com